A CENTURY O...

COLIN R...

This book travels through both the 19th and 20th centuries charting the struggles faced by Dockworkers. They probably had the worse employers that existed throughout our country. I would like to thank Tony Banfield for his contribution and his support in urging me on to complete the story.

I dedicate this book to my Father where he was a character in London's Royal Docks. He invented the art of survival.

Introduction

It's hard knowing where to start in trying to explain the hardships that Dockworkers experienced for almost a hundred years. The struggle to get a decent wage and therefore escape the poverty trap was brought to the public's notice when the great strike of 1889 better known as "the dockers tanner strike" took place. This strike pricked the consciences of people who generally held the labouring classes in very low regard.

Taking into account that this struggle was some 125 years ago there was no internet, no mobile telephones in fact the telephone had only been invented some 10 years prior to this struggle and only the very rich could even think of having this new gadget installed in their homes. So for the working classes communication would be made by telegram or a person who would be dispatched to carry the message to whoever it was designated for.

The poverty that existed in dock neighbourhoods was widespread with living conditions so bad that Parliamentarian's although doing nothing to eradicate the problem frequently referred to the problem as a serious problem on our conscience. This book mainly explains the struggles and living conditions centred all around the East

End of London but they represent similar conditions that all Britain's major ports faced.

This book makes no apologies for its attack on the shipping companies, the dock employers and lastly but most certainly not least of all the conservative governments who were working in tandem with the ship-owners and the port employers. The dreadful social and working conditions were only allowed to exist because of the tory government's failure to introduce legislation to call a halt to the conditions that prevailed in an industry that helped maintain Britain's place as a leader in exporting goods to almost every country in the World making this country the richest nation on earth.

Finally I have called this book A Century of Struggle and as you take the trip through the book I hope you will understand why I chose this title. You will be able to make your mind up as to whether the port employers were the worst employers in the industrial field. They were strict employers in Victorian times and continued these values right up into the nineteen sixties.

The Dockers Tanner

Most people who belonged to the working classes in the 19th century worked from dawn to dusk for seven days a week had no rights or trade unions representing them, the employer was god it was he who told you what your lot in life would be. Even when there might have been a position of a labour shortage- although this hardly ever happened the bosses stuck to their rigid working terms and refused to increase wages which might have attracted workers to fill any vacancies.

Given these conditions you might have thought that the dockworkers were in the same boat as the rest of the working classes. Well if you know of any industry that had to endure these conditions then the author would be grateful if you could contact him with the details. In the meantime history shows that the conditions imposed on dockworkers at the time were nothing short of barbaric.

The job started with the call on- this was where a dockworker shaped for work. Thousands of causal workers would have the same idea so the foreman would parade up and down the swelled ranks of men choosing who he thought was the fittest for the job he had to offer, men desperate for work would surge forward trampling over men who had been knocked over in the panic for a job, anyone could shape for a job so often had the position of tens of thousands of men trying for a couple of hundred jobs.

If you had been successful in getting a job your troubles had just started as many of the men were so poor that they had not eaten for over 24 hours and they were so weak that they could not carry out the strenuous working conditions that was expected of them. Many just did an hours work and took the 5 old pennies (2p in modern money) for the hours work that they had done. This was then spent on getting some food so as they could once again shape on the call in the hope of securing another job. The foreman or the ship worker had the right to hire and fire whenever he felt the occasion warranted such action.

Working conditions left a great deal to be desired as there was no mechanisation of any description to assist the loading or unloading of cargos. Many of which were in hessian bags or cardboard boxes and contained dangerous commodities, that led to serious health issues. The only tools that assisted the dockworker was the dockers hook this gave the person using it an extension of his reach and was able to grip the box or bale more easily.

Once the day's work had been completed the dockworker who by now would be thoroughly exhausted would return home which would in all probability be a single room or at best he would share a house with another family. This could see up to 20 people living in a 2 up 2 down terraced house. Then he would come face to face with reality when the wife had prepared a meal from whatever she could lay her hands on given that money was desperately short. Once that you reached an age where you could no longer carry out such arduous tasks it was the poor house for you if your children were not able to support you.

Taking all this into account you can understand why after the famous victory that the Bryant & May match girls had recently achieved that men were beginning to listen to people about joining trade unions. Such a union was already in existence and its leader was a man who came from a humble background Ben Tillet. He had joined a union called the tea operatives and general labourers association. He had attended evening classes to further his education and at the age of 27 he was elected general secretary of the union. Within a year of being elected he led a strike at Tilbury Docks which ended in defeat for Tillet and his members. He gave serious consideration to giving it all up but he was persuaded to carry on and what he did next is history.

He then decided that that in order to defeat the dock employers he needed a much larger union so he recruited as many unskilled labourers as he could. He then named this union the Dock Wharf, Riverside and General Workers Union. It would be this union that would spearhead the greatest strike that had ever taken place in the 1890s. On August the 12th a ship discharging in the West India Docks would spark off a strike that would be famously known as the Docker's tanner.

The ship in question was the Lady Armstrong and the normal practise of paying the men "plus money" for completing the work quicker than was expected was withdrawn. The men stopped work when they heard that the employers had withdrawn it because they stated that it had been withdrawn in order to keep costs down, thus giving them a chance to attract more ships.

Tillet wasted no time he instructed the men to picket the docks and although only 500 men from the West India and East India Docks marched out within a few days the stevedores union threw their weight behind the dockworkers claims. This was a turning point as the stevedores were looked upon as superior to the casual dockworkers and as the stevedores only loaded ships they not only ground the port to a complete standstill but their general secretary issued a leaflet calling on all trades to support the claim. Within 7 days some 30,000 men were out on strike and the figure was growing.

Ben Tillet knew that he required funds if the struggle was to be kept going so he set about forming what was to become a very formidable strike committee, firstly he made Tom Mann his first lieutenant and gave him the unenviable task of raising funds so as the strikers could get some help towards feeding their families. Mann quickly enrolled Eleanor Marx, wife of Karl Marx and Will Thorne the gas workers union leader to assist him in galvanising as much help as was required. The Salvation Army threw its hall open to dockworkers and their families and they supplied some 10,000 loaves of bread every day.

Other church halls followed suit although not on the scale of the Salvation Army they all provided a service that was invaluable to the striking dockworkers and their families. One such church leader and a local councillor to offer his services was John Benn who would eventually become the M.P for Tower Hamlets. He was the first of four generations of Benn's to serve as M.Ps his son William Benn married Lily Pickstone who was a distant relation to the Wedgewood Pottery family so William Benn added the name by deed poll and we have the Wedgewood-Benn dynasty.

Probably Tillets shrewdest move was to get John Burns on the strike committee although Burns was known as a radical and had been imprisoned for incitement he could deliver speeches like no one else, his support was essential to deliver speeches praising the men up for their gallantry in continuing the strike despite widespread poverty but his greatest asset was to blast away at the dock companies. The chairman of the East India Dock Company had made a speech in which he stated that he would starve the men into submission and they would gladly return to work on the old terms.

Both Burns and Tillet seized upon this and Tillet made a speech in which he stated that he wished the chairman to be dead-he later had to withdraw this however the employers remark stating that they would starve the men into submission was never retracted.

Typically it was a retired service man that kicked of the strike in the West India Docks he was Lieutenant Colonel John Lowther du Platt who was general manager of the East and West India Dock Company. Like many of his counterparts he was appointed after a distinguished military career however what he knew about dock work and the hardships faced by dockworkers and their families could be fitted on the back of a postage stamp.

Another politician who decided to enter the affray by

financially backing a group who were actively getting scab labour to work the strike bound ships was Randolph Churchill, in keeping with the Churchill families dislike of the working classes he ploughed the families money into a group who were hell bent on smashing the dockworkers. But there you have the Churchill family they would contribute to smash trade unions but they would rather be seen dead before helping out a working class movement.

It might be worth pointing out at this early stage as to why so many men shaped for work in the docks despite the wretched conditions and the bad rates of pay, for many unskilled labourers the docks offered them the only chance of securing a day's work, many of these labourers had little or no educational skills whatsoever. In all probability they had left school at the age of 10 or 11 to get a messengers job in an effort to bring some much needed money to their home. However this would ensure that their future held no prospects whatsoever. In short they had been sentenced to a life of purgatory.

They were caught in the trap and the ruling classes were determined that this supply of unskilled labour would continue and as a result the social and working conditions would be left unchanged for years. The strike was growing in size as the strike entered the second week but the strike committee knew that unless funds were to come in then the employers words of starving the men back to work would ring true. It was John Burns who suggested that a mass march right through the heart of London to draw attention to the plight of the striking men.

An American reporter who had never seen scenes

like it sent a cable back to his newspaper which was owned by William Randolph Hearst the newspaper tycoon in both New York and San Francisco. The reporter stated in his article that he had never seen anything so wretched in his life he carried on by saying that unless help was immediately forthcoming then one of life's biggest atrocities would take place. Hearst vetoed the article and ultimately decided to publish it.

Yet no help was forthcoming from the American longshoremen (that's their name for dockworkers) it would be the Australian wharfies (dockers) who would turn the tide of the strike. When they heard of the plight of the London dockers and their families they cabled funds over immediately. Many of the Australian wharfies had been transported to Australia and they knew of the conditions facing the striking men. In all they sent some £30,000 which in today's terms would be worth some three million pounds!

But before this magnificent effort from Australia the marchers marched through London into Leadenhall Street where the ship-owners had their main offices up into Whitehall where the seat of Government was and they collected much needed funds. Back in the strike hit areas the shop keepers were giving limited tick to regular customers and the church was throwing their weight behind the strikers by opening every available hall to serve soup and bread to help bring some relief to the striking families. Burns and Mann now had some funds in which they could distribute to the men, they issued tokens that could be exchanged in local shops.

The strike committee drew up a list of demands before they would consider returning to work and the main plank of their demands was an increase in the hourly rate from 5d an hour to 6d the famous Docker's tanner. Also included in the demands was that overtime rates be increased from 6d an hour to 8d an hour. The strike committee demanded that any man engaged for work be guaranteed 4 hours as opposed to the hourly hire and fire method that was currently in operation. They also demanded that the number of call ons be reduced to 2 call ons a day.

The employer's response to these demands was to reject them out of hand. Tillet knew that he had to keep the moral of the men at a level that the strike remained as solid as it was, despite the fact that blackleg labour being brought in the strike had paralysed the port of London. Only the odd ship was being worked by blackleg labour who knew nothing about loading and unloading ships. The relief fund was now able to issue tokens to every dockworker to obtain some food and clothing from shops that took part in the scheme. The dock employers for the first time detected that they might lose this struggle and for the first time there were mutterings of discontent between the shipping companies and some of the dock employers.

One of the main stays of the strike committee was Will Crooks who was delegated to address the men at the East India Docks his oratory was a good as anyone else on the organising committee he was another one who hailed from working class stock and the men held him in high regard, he was respected for his forthright views and it was this that gained him the total respect of the men.

Many factories in and around the dock area were coming out on strike in support of the dockworkers and by August 27th it was estimated that a 130.000 people were on strike. The tide had turned and on one of the mass marches which was preceded by large brass bands the office workers all rushed out to give donations to the dockworkers to help ease the hardships. This was too much for some of the employers to bear and just like rats fleeing a sinking ship some of them indicated to the strike committee that they would consider opening talks with a view to ending the strike at their wharf.

But a new development took place as the dispute entered its fourth week with the Lord Mayor of London forming the Mansion House committee. This committee that included Cardinal Manning the Archbishop of Westminster who never hid where his loyalties laid and that was with the strikers. The objective of this committee was to bring the 2 sides together in an attempt to end the dispute. But as this committee was taking evidence from both sides dock companies who could sense defeat were meeting with members of the strike committee to negotiate a deal that would ensure that workers would return at the owner's wharfs.

The first to break ranks from the employers rigid stance was a Henry Lafone who was the general manager of Butlers Wharf, he had paid his 300 men a shilling a day whilst the strike was on and he paid this on Saturday and Sundays to. He settled up with the strike committee and before long his wharf was working normally. The shipowners were now getting fed up with some of the dock companies who were still refusing to accept that they would have to concede certain points to the strike committee and it was when the ship owners announced that they might form their own companies to unload and load their ships.

This brought the dock companies scurrying to the Mansion House committee as they did not want to lose the contract that was making them vast sums of money. There were some 250 dock companies operating in London with some of them unloading just one ship a year giving them enough money to live the grand lifestyle that they were accustomed to unlike the poor souls who they employed to unload the ship that they had contracted to do.

When it came to the Mansion House Committee to deliver its verdict Cardinal Manning had managed to convince the other members to grant the dockworkers the 6d per hour, 8d per hour for overtime, a guaranteed 4 hours work once a man had been engaged, the main concession was the recognition of the unions, however the strike committees demand that the plus payments be abolished was neither rejected nor conceded but they recommended that another committee be set up to look at this and some other points that the strikers were demanding.

This was nothing short of a total victory for the dockworkers who then held mass marches throughout the capital ending with Tillet addressing the men proclaiming that the men's actions had brought the employers to heel.

Tillet once again renamed the union this time it would be known as the Dock, Wharf, Riverside and General Workers Union. Within a few months of the victory the new union had recruited some 20,000 new members.

Many of the people who were involved in organising the strike and offering assistance to the strikers would go on to higher office. Tillet contested 2 parliamentary elections before being elected as an independent M.P in 1917 at the Salford by election, he had left the Labour party after failing to get on with Keir Hardie and Ramsay McDonald because of his stance as a pro war delegate, he advocated bombing German civilian areas and that pacifists should be severely punished this left him almost friendless within the Labour movement.

In contrast to Tillet John Burns became a M.P for Battersea in 1892 for the Liberal Party and was to become one of the first working class members to hold a cabinet post however his anti-war stance saw him resign from the government in 1914 in protest at Britain joining the war against Germany. Possibly the exception to the rule was Tom Mann who refused to give up his communist beliefs and continued to hold many posts in trade unions and trade councils.

John Benn would become M.P for Tower Hamlets in 1892 and so the Benn dynasty was born. He was Knighted in 1906 and made a baronet in 1914. The one person who would fall foul of everyone was Will Crooks he like most of the strike committee would become an M.P for Woolwich in 1902 however he started out by falling out in 1911 with the T.U.C over a remark he made regarding disabled persons whom he described as human vermin, this really wasn't the shrewdest of moves and when he supported this countries involvement in world war 1 that put paid to his chances of high office as most of the senior members of the labour party were anti-war.

What is noticeable even at the turn of the 19th century was that most of the leaders all took jobs as M.Ps or became senior figures within the trade union movement. However the difference between these men and the more modern day leaders is that people like Tillet, Crooks and Burns were pioneers for the working classes who had no-one in Parliament to represent them.

But whilst all the leaders were having their heads turned by the chance of securing higher office the lot of the dockworker remained very much the same other than the wage increase that had been secured the conditions were still appallingly bad, the call on although it had now been restricted to 2 call ons a day still resembled a cattle market with the foreman marching up and down amongst men who were so desperate for work that they forgot that they were human beings and would fight and trample over fellow workers in a desperate effort to get the foreman to give them a job.

Furthermore the dock companies and the ship-owners were still smarting from what was the biggest defeat and more importantly the real birth of the trade union movement, the bosses were not going to allow that to happen again. They started to draw up plans to ensure such an event would never be allowed to occur again the first of which was the formation of the British Shipping

Federation in 1890, this was what could be best described as the shipping companies own trade union, every British ship-owners would be members and there would be no repeat of the last strike where individual companies started to do deals on their own.

Added to this was the fact that the dock companies and stevedoring contractors knew that if they broke ranks like some of them did in the last strike then the shipping companies would ensure that they would not get the contracts to work their vessels. As the years rolled by the lot of the dockworkers never got any better and with prices increasing the dockworkers found themselves in a worse position than they were in over 10 years ago.

Many workers were in the same boat when it came to rates of pay and as a consequence in the summer of 1911 a rash of strikes broke out the first and probably the most effective was the seaman's strike which started in Liverpool and quickly spread. When the shipping companies realised how effective and disruptive the strike was they quickly conceded the claim to the seamen. Other groups took note and before long nearly all the transport workers were engaged in strikes to achieve better rates of pay. Liverpool was the centre of this dispute with the whole city practically engaged in strikes; it was so bad that Churchill ordered 2 gun boats up the River Mersey. London dockers decided that they should join in as they had not seen their pay increased since the 1889 strike again the companies conceded to the demands of increasing the basic hourly rate of pay to 8d an hour.

This was what the dockworker's where up against

Tillet knew that he faced an employer who never forgave him or the dockworkers for the 1889 defeat. Not only had they not awarded any rise whatsoever since that strike but wherever possible they had enforced their own set of conditions and they most certainly never benefited the wellbeing of the dockworkers. Abstract poverty was still widespread amongst all dockland communities, but as always they stuck together and helped each other out when times become really desperate.

Probably the greatest example of why the ship-owners and dock employers should be known as robber barons occurred during this struggle. The ship Lady Jocelyn was brought to the strike hit docks with a cargo of strike breakers, they would be transported under guard to the ships that were being worked and after they finished they would be returned to the Lady Jocelyn for a meal and board, this was all paid for by the shipping federation. This ship had a dubious career as a ship its history included bringing back the soldiers from the Indian mutiny uprising, then the ship was used to ferry troops to bring about an end to the second Maori uprising in New Zealand.

The strike breakers had been recruited from as far afield as Holland and they had been promised 30 shillings a week with free board and lodgings, the shipping federation even hired the steamer Clacton Belle every Sunday to ferry 800 blacklegs on a 5 hour cruise up the Thames with free booze and baccy thrown in! If only they had treated the dockworkers with part of the conditions that they were offering the scabs then perhaps the strike may have been unnecessary.

Tillet and his strike committee somehow managed to get the employers to agree a settlement whereby the employers agreed to pay the 8d an hour, however a soon as the return to work took place a minority of dock employers started implementing the old rates and gradually other dock employers started to follow suit. Their argument was that if they paid the new rates it would give other employers paying the old rates the edge in competition. Port Employers stated that they would have to close down their businesses if they were forced to pay the new rates.

1912 wasn't the greatest of years for Britain. The suffragettes were protesting and getting themselves arrested and imprisoned whilst one of the main leaders Sylvia Pankhurst formed the first women's suffragettes' movement in East London. The Titanic sunk with a terrible loss of life and Captain Scott reached the South Pole only to discover that someone had already got there before him and as is that wasn't bad enough he and all his team perished.

Meanwhile the labouring classes could take no more they had seen the cost of living increase over the past 2 years which meant that in real terms their already poor wages had further decreased. Then In what would turn out to be a disastrous move the new union decided to throw their weight behind the striking Lightermen who had struck for more pay. This was a strike that would turn out to be a defeat that remained in dockworkers memories right up until the closure of the docks.

Firstly the employers now led by the chairman of the

Port of London Authority Lord Devonport decided that although they had in the main reneged on the previous agreement that ended the 1911 strike that they would not negotiate while men were refusing to work. Tillet and the up and coming Ernest Bevin decided to take the dock companies on. The strike saw Winston Churchill employ troops and strike breakers with police being armed to ensure that the convoys of army trucks reached the wholesale markets intact.

    As the strike went on things got even bitterer. The employers began putting out statements condemning the strikers and reiterating their position of refusing to negotiate a settlement. This had all the hallmarks of the 1889 strike with all the poverty and hardship that went with it. As the strike continued in London with some reports giving an estimated 100,000 men out on strike the robber barons dug their heels in and the chairman of the Port of London Authority who was leading the dock employers totally ignored the Prime Ministers request that they meet with the unions and bring the strike to a close.

    Unfortunately for the striking London dockworkers support was not forthcoming from workers in other ports and Churchill once again introduced troops and police along with strike breakers who had been brought from all corners of the country and were afforded heavy police and troops protection to stop striking dockworkers getting anywhere near them. Tillet like many who followed in his footsteps had taken his eye of off the main issue for a few months earlier he along with some other fellow socialists had launched the Daily Herald a national newspaper giving the workers point of view.

There was no assistance from outside like they had received in the great tanner strike London men were isolated and Devonport knew it and he continued to wade in with speeches meant to provoke both the men and their leaders in fact Tillet speaking at a mass rally on Tower Hill was so enraged by Devonport's attitude that he led a prayer asking the lord to strike Lord Devonport dead! This provoked an angry response from both the media and the employers and Tillet was forced to retract the statement although in retracting he stated that wishing Lord Devonport dead might be seen as harsh to some people but to the men he represented they agreed with such a request.

The East End community spirit tried its best to rally round and give support to the dockworkers and their families with the Jewish tailors playing a sterling role by throwing their homes open to dockworkers that were without homes and they also threw their homes open where the dockworkers and their families could get a meal. Once again the churches and the Salvation Army tried their best in offering assistance to the striking families but it was a task that could not be met due to the numbers involved.

The Government had commissioned Sir Edward Clarke to look into both sides grievances and the hastily prepared report came firmly down on the dockworkers side. Clarke reported that there was overwhelming evidence that the dock companies had not implemented the award that they had agreed in ending the previous year's strike. The robber barons were now summoned to attend the Board of Trade offices to discuss the report. However the Wharfingers Association and the Port of London Authority both refused to attend the meeting and issued a press release stating that by their non-attendance they would not be party to any decisions that may have been made.

They went on to say that they felt they had been forced into the previous year's settlement and that if they were to pay the wage increase then the shareholders would in all probability lose their dividends for that year! It beggars belief that such a statement could be put out showing concern for a few fat cats whilst there was human suffering on a scale that had not been seen since the 1889 strike.

Tillet now knew that the odds were heavily stacked against his men and to make matters worse the suffering that the men were enduring had seen some men join the scabs in returning to work. What had forced these men to break ranks and joins the blackleg labour doesn't bear thinking about for in docklands there is nothing lower than a scab. These men had to endure the taunts of being called scabs and blacklegs for the rest of their lives and even some of their sons were forced to share their father's fate. It never went away once a scab it would go to the grave with you. As if this wasn't bad enough some 2 years after the strike had ended dockworkers rioted and attacked shops that had been friendly to strike-breakers.

So the Robber Barons had lived up to their name, they had refused to talk to the men's accredited trade unions, they had ignored pleas from the Government to enter talks with a view to bring about an end to the struggle. The Government had even agreed with the men on strike that the dock companies should have honoured the 1911 agreement and as such paid the men the correct rates of pay. But the shipping federation was having none of it and despite some 100,000 men being on strike they continued their approach of refusing to attend talks while the men were on strike.

Such was the hatred that both the ship-owners and the Conservative Government showed to the dockworkers and their unions that at a mass rally in Liverpool where Tom Mann was addressing a huge meeting the police drew their truncheons and made an attack on the crowd leaving scores of dockworkers badly injured and many more running for their lives.

This was not the first time that dockworkers had felt the full force of the law because in 1890 police made a bayonette charge on Southampton dockworkers then in 1893 Dockworkers in Fetherstone during a miners strike police under Government orders opened fire and shot and killed 2 miners with many more injured.

The church had once again tried to intervene on behalf of the men to try and end the suffering that had been brought about by the dispute however again the dock companies remained rock solid in refusing any attempt of conciliation. One man emerged from the carnage to rise to greater heights as a direct result of what he had witnessed and he was Ernest Bevin.

He later stated that the suffering that the

dockworkers had endured would remain with him for the rest of his life, he had witnessed the ship-owners and dock companies treating human beings as if they were sewer rats. Bevin never forgot this strike and swore that he would revenge this terrible atrocity that the employers had created by their dogmatic attitude of firstly reneging on an agreement and secondly almost forcing the men into action for 10 weeks in trying to secure what was rightfully theirs.

On July 28th the strike committee finally called a halt to the strike. A unanimous decision to return to work with immediate effect was passed by the strike committee, they knew that the Government whilst trying to conciliate were using police and troops to protect the scab labour that the shipping federation had recruited up and down the country. The union called on the employer's to honour all agreements and conditions that had been in place prior to the dispute adding that there should be no victimisation against strikers who were involved in organising in keeping the strike going.

Upon the resumption of work Tillet and Bevan secured the 8d an hour for their members! It beggars belief that an employer would allow total starvation and unimaginable suffering that went on for 10 weeks just to teach the labour force a lesson. Many of the strike leaders found themselves blacklisted and the only jobs that they could find was the type of job that no-one wanted as it would be dirty, hazardous and did not pay as much as normal jobs. The "normal" rate of 8d per hour would be equivalent to earning £1.50 an hour today; this highlights how poorly the dockworkers were paid.

Phrases being used by both Government Ministers and dock employer's accused the striking dockworkers of being unpatriotic and holding the British public to ransom although there was no reference from the Government as to the actions adopted by the shipping federation who were acting on behalf of both the shipping companies and the dock employers. The relationship between the dock companies and the dockworkers had now hit an all-time low. Union membership dropped dramatically as many of the dockworkers believed that what was the point of being in a union after a catastrophic defeat that had lasted 10 weeks and left them even poorer than they were before.

History has a strange knack for portraying the events that suited the ruling classes as many historians show this period as the Edwardian Era which according to the authors of these times frequently refer to this period as a time of peace and plenty. Obviously the historians missed out covering the dock areas up and down the country or else the Edwardian Era might best be remembered as the time of peace and poverty for the majority of the population.

Tillet and Bevin began the mammoth task of rebuilding and strengthening the union so as there could never be a repeat of what had recently occurred. Bevan who had now been appointed national organiser of the union began talks with other unions with a view to amalgamating everyone into one large union so as they could match employers organisations such as the shipping federation. He was not a union leader who had a privileged education nor did he hanker for a huge home in a fashionable area in fact he left school at the age of 11 to start work as a labourer. But the First World War was about to intervene which led to plans of merging many smaller unions into one large union had to be put on the back burner.

But before all this could take place Tillet had become besotted with the idea of becoming an M.P. 4 times he stood as a Parliamentary candidate and 4 times he was unsuccessful before securing the Salford North seat in 1917. However this was to be his undoing and because he made a speech supporting the war and condemning pacifists he found himself at odds with many of the same people who had supported him in all of the struggles that had taken place in the docks. Ultimately it would cost him the leadership of the great union merger that would take place later.

In his memoirs Lloyd George firmly believed that in the spring and summer of 1914 strikes of an unparalleled nature was about to explode in British industries. Workers were beginning to join the trade unions again to get their wretched working conditions and rates of pay increased. Perhaps this explains why this country could not wait to enter the war in that year. All of a sudden instead of referring striking workers as unpatriotic and enemies of the country the same voices were now calling on every abled bodied men to take up arms and fight for your country.

Even though the war was conducted mainly in France with thousands of men being butchered every day the Germans tried their level best to bomb London's docks with their zeppelin airships. In the main they were blown of target by high winds and in one attack instead of dropping their bombs over London's docks they ended up bombing Great Yarmouth. But in France the killings continued which would lead to a dreadful shortage of men able to carry out manual work once the war was over.

In the ever increasing need for more young men to join up and be shipped to France to join the war all talk of working men who only a couple of years earlier where being branded unpatriotic and enemies of the state were quickly forgotten as thousands of dockworkers and other labourers from the working classes joined up and went on to perform some heroic acts of bravery. These boys were most certainly not unpatriotic or traitors.

Ironically the war although now over had a final sting in its tail, the wretched conditions in the trenches had become a breeding ground for a virus that was believed to have emanated from rats. It was the Spanish Flu and it was responsible for more deaths that there had been in the whole of the war. The virus had been brought home from the trenches and death was sudden you could get up in the morning and feel a slight twinge by lunch time your skin would have turned purple and you would be dead by tea time. This added to the intense shortage of workers needed to rebuild the economy.

However despite there being an acute shortage of labour which would in normal times lead to workers calling the shots and as a result the employers would have to increase wages in order to be able to keep a labour force that would enable the employer to run their business smoothly. Strangely enough this never happened with dock labourers they seemed to have picked up where they left of as did the dock companies who carried on treating their employees as if they were animals.

The conditions in the docks were as wretched as they had ever been but although wages and conditions were in the main worse than what most labouring workers were receiving this never stopped the ship-owners and the Port of London Authority rapidly expanding the docks and jetties in an attempt to attract even more shipping to what was the trading capital of the world.

There were over 500 different wharfs based all along the Thames as far up river as Brentford stretching right down to Tilbury. These wharfs would specialise in the types of cargoes that they handled which would usually require a regular labour force that knew how to handle certain cargoes without causing damage to the goods. As you travelled along the River Thames the congestion of small ships and lighters waiting to collect the cargoes was so bad that it almost made it impossible to work out how the ships and lighters ever managed to weave their way onto the berth.

However, even back in those times the shipping companies and the merchants who owned the goods, where far from happy with the amount of pilfering that was taking place in the wharves. River pirates were the main culprits once they ascertained how valuable a cargo was then during the night they would travel along the river and steal as much as their craft could carry. Security was almost non-existent and rather than address the problem many ship-owners started to look elsewhere and so the boom period of constructing new docks began.

Today the outcry would be so loud that it would not be possible to get away with it but back in the 19th and early 20th century you would find warehouses stuffed full of cargoes such as elephant tusks, thousands of them meeting the demand for the ivory trade, furs from animals that would become extinct because of the slaughtering that took place to obtain a precious fur. Ostrich feathers by the thousand, turtles in cold store awaiting to be used for state banquets. Again there was rare timber that had seen trees chopped down that had taken centuries to grow only to see timber merchants wiping out strains of trees in the name of profit.

The dock that had the most upriver location was Brentford Dock and it was reckoned that this dock handled 10% of all of Britain's trade via small ships and barges that handled an immense amount of trade adding to this was the fact that factories based in South East England would send their produce to the docks via Brentford Dock.

Whilst Brentford Dock was the furthermost upriver dock in the opposite direction was the new Port of Tilbury, this was constructed to save ships spending best part of a day sailing along the River Thames to reach whatever dock or wharf that they required to unload their cargo. With all this redevelopment taking place the dock companies found themselves in fierce competition with each other and the main sufferers were as always the dockworkers.

Each wharf and the various docks usually had regular trades that they specialized in if you took the Surrey

Commercial Docks you knew that in the main they unloaded timber and paper from Canada and the Scandinavian countries. There was so much timber that you wondered if there were any trees left. Then you had the West India Docks that had been constructed by merchants who owned sugar plantations in Jamaica, they were outraged at the amount of pilfering that was taking place along the wharfs. So a request to Parliament and the West India Docks was born and it would mainly trade in sugar, rum and other exotic cargoes that emanated from the West Indies.

  Another piece of waste land was quickly gobbled up by merchants wanting their own docks and the Millwall Docks was born which would mainly trade in grain and timber however the merchants somehow managed to fall foul of the Government and the rights to operate a bonded warehouse was withdrawn which in turn led to a decline in trade and ultimately led to the Millwall Dock merging into the West India Docks.

  Then there was the East India Docks which again was paid for and constructed by a group of merchants who were trading in the East Indies. Tea would be their major import and given that tea was a luxury that only the upper classes could afford the need for strict security and a bonded warehouse was the order of the day along with the tea came spices and silks that these merchants had picked up for a pittance in the East Indies and in turn would make them fortunes.

  The largest dock by far was the Royal Docks which were soon to become even larger with the construction of the King Gorge V Dock which would join up with the Royal Victoria Dock and the Royal Albert Dock. With this additional dock the Royal Docks would become the world's largest enclosed docks. Such was the trade Britain had her Empire and London was the gateway to it. Mores the pity that the men who would help make the country rich and powerful were not given any of the spoils.

The Aftermath of the War

Following on from the war was the fact that despite the huge loss of life, which in turn created a shortage of able bodied men able to carry out heavy industrial work which in normal circumstances would usually lead to higher wages saw inflation creeping up which in turn eroded even further into the dockworkers and other labouring workers already poor wages.

Despite the magnificent job that women had done during the war by working flat out in munition factories and in many other fields that had become vacant as a result of most of the men being used in the war they quickly discovered that despite all the praise that had been heaped upon them for carrying out these tasks they were quickly forgotten and the attitude of the bosses was thanks a lot and goodbye!

Strikes broke out right across the whole spectrum of many industries which gave the Government cause to link the trouble to the recent revolution that had recently occurred in Russia. The Daily Mail even went as far as to publishing a letter from one of the leaders of the Russian revolution to the leader of the T.U.C stating that they should back strikes and that may lead to the overthrow of the British Government. The letter was later found to be a forgery but the damage had been done in printing it. This is a practise that was widely used by the newspaper publishers to make sure that public sympathy would not be repeated as it was in the great strike of 1889.

Many countries including Britain were in financial

trouble as a result of paying for the war which in turn led to a downturn in world trade. Once again as in any slump or depression the first in the firing line would be dockworkers as the need for men to unload and load ships waned. This would once again heap yet more misery and poverty in areas that were already best described as slums with most houses being used to house as many families as the landlord could get away with. This led to living conditions that contributed to disease and conditions that would not be tolerated in any shape or form these days.

Winston Churchill came up with another brainstorm by joining the gold standard in 1925 he as Chancellor of the Exchequer stated that by re-joining the gold standard Britain once again would be great. All very good if you had pots of money but the truth of Churchill's monumental mistake was that trade was already in the doldrums and by joining the gold standard the pound was fixed at 4.25 dollars to the British pound. This made our exports even dearer. If you look at the consequences of Churchill's move it would be the contributing factor for the great depression that was to follow in the 1930s.

Yes society might put Churchill on a pedestal as one of the world's greatest statesman but he made some monumental mistakes right throughout his life that were both economically disastrous and in times of war would lead to the death of thousands of men. Added to this was the fact the both he and his family had an inbred hatred of the working classes. In the East End of London Churchill was not universally held in high regard.

Meanwhile the Dock, Wharf, Riverside & General

Workers Union saw that the only way that the atrocious working conditions could be tackled once and for all was by registering every Dockworker, this was fiercely opposed by the employers who saw that the existing conditions favoured them and as such they would go to any lengths to oppose new working conditions. Bevin by now was the rising star in the union and it was he who drew up a set of demands to present to the employers that included a guaranteed daily payment of sixteen shillings, a registration scheme to be given priority, added to the claim was a clause that stated that maintenance should also be given special consideration, this was reference to a complete change in the working conditions that prevailed. Bevin also called upon the employers to introduce a scheme whereby the employers had to introduce special light duties that the older dockworkers could perform.

    It came as no surprise when the employers played for time and started referring certain aspects of the dockers claim to various other committees which would drag out the claim, and, as the employers hoped would lead to the dockworkers settling for far less than they had originally claimed. Bevin was having none of it and after a judicial enquiry that had come down firmly on the dockworkers side still the employers tried to wriggle out of the obligations that they had been recommended to implement.

    So the Ministry of Labour along with the Board of Trade set up the Shaw enquiry this was to be the forerunner of many enquiries that various Governments set up in an attempt to buy peace in an industry that was becoming an embarrassment to the British capitalist system.

The employers immediately engaged the best council that money could buy to present their evidence to the Shaw enquiry whilst Bevin would lead the union's case for major reform within the industry. It would be Bevin who wiped the floor with the legal counsel that the shipping federation had engaged, he called for a scheme whereby every dockworker would be registered which would bring about an end to the barbaric conditions that the employers had imposed upon the dockworkers. Newspapers gave the enquiry front page coverage and once again because of Bevin's articulate speeches to the Shaw enquiry the public symphonised with the dockworkers this had not happened since the 1889 dispute and the Shaw report and the Government did not know how to get out of the mess.

Once again despite the Shaw enquiry recommending that wholesale changes should be made the employers along with their Conservative friends found methods that would slow down any possible progress that would be made as a result of the enquiries recommendations, because none of the recommendations had been accepted another committee headed by Sir Donald Maclean was set up and the whole question of the disastrous working conditions that prevailed in the dock industry was once again given an airing. The main issue was that of giving the dockworkers a registration.

By now Bevin had seen enough of the employers and their continuing stalling tactics and was instrumental in merging many unions into one giant union. This union would be known as the Transport and General Workers Union with Bevin becoming the General Secretary. Despite this he was still finding it difficult to get the ship-owners and the stevedoring contractors to agree to the most basic of demands. They had conceded to paying the men eight shillings per half a day but when it came down to paying them wages for not being able to find work well this was a different matter.

The employers believed that they had conceded far too much in paying the 8 shillings per half a day in wages coupled with an increase in some of the piece work rates along with a general increase in overtime rates plus provision for the men to take a dinner break! The sheer audacity of the employers leaves you absolutely speechless! They considered by allowing the men to knock off for an unpaid dinner break was a concession, also the overtime rates had not been increased for years and they also considered this to be a further concession.

However when it came down to granting the men a full registration and paying the men unemployment pay this was a definite no no. Bevin had believed that following the Shaw enquiry he was almost home and dry on the question of every dockworker getting a registration. He was so confident that he got some 61,000 men who were working as causal labourers to submit their names on a register in readiness for any such scheme that would be introduced. Little did Bevin know that it would be another 24 years before the dockworkers gained a registration and that he would be the architect of the 1947 dock labour scheme that was to be introduced under a Labour

Government.

    The employers tried every trick in the book to convince dockworkers that any scheme that led to the introduction of a registration would be more harmful than beneficial to the dockworkers. They warned regular workers that they stood to lose any advantage that they held at present and that the cost of such a scheme would drive many employers into bankruptcy. What they conveniently overlooked was the fact that the call on system for causal workers was so disgraceful that many of their own friends who were large employers of labour looked upon the call system on as an embarrassment that the capitalist system could well do without. More important than the few regulars who may have held semi regular jobs with certain shipping lines were the tens of thousands of men who never enjoyed this luxury and a registration would certainly benefit them.

    For these unfortunate men they would go down to whatever dock that they thought might give them a chance of a few days' work, having got there they then had to face the indignity of fighting amongst themselves in an attempt to attract them to the foreman who was trying to select the best men available to man the job that he was responsible for. As was the case more often than not most of the men who had failed to secure a job then had to return home penniless. They had set out hungry and they were going to return home even more hungry.

    The Shaw enquiry although it had not initially been set up to enquire into the causal system in the docks could not help but be impressed with the evidence that Bevin had given and they urged all parties within the dock industry to address the urgent matter of ending the casual system as a matter of priority. The employer's response was to set up another committee that would gradually brush the whole issue under the carpet. More and more committees and enquiries were put in place by various Governments to deal with the issue but as before the employers either stalled or completely ignored any findings that did not suit them. In fact it would take another 20 years and another world war before any semblance of a registration was introduced for the dockworkers.

In fact following the Shaw Enquiry in 1920 the employers stalling tactics forced both the Unions and the Government to set up further committees and inquiries in an attempt to force the dock employers to change their attitudes towards the people they employed. The next enquiry was held in 1924 under the chairmanship of Donald Maclean M.P which was followed by a Departmental enquiry into Port Labour that dragged on right through 1930 into the following year. Again all found that conditions needed to be changed but the employers still resisted all the pressure that was applied.

Yet another committee was set up under the guise of the Standing Advisory Committee for the Port Transport Industry this was made up of representatives from both the unions and employers but once again they failed to agree on introducing a scheme that would abolish the casual system. If you thought 20 years was a long time to wait before the dockworkers won their registration then it would take over 35 years before the casual system was abolished. However the great depression of the 1930s saw more and more labourers without work turning up at the docks in an attempt to get some work, this only added more men to the already vastly inflated numbers of men seeking work. So the employers had to introduce some kind of register to ensure that the men who were trying to obtain work were regular dockworkers who had a pretty good idea of how to unload a ship or indeed how to stow cargo whilst loading ships. But still the employers resisted the idea of a full registration scheme. Talk about wanting your cake and eating it.

Bevin now knew that the only way that these employers would give the men a registration and a fair deal would be by introducing an act of Parliament and thereby forcing a scheme onto these employers he also recognised that the Conservative's whilst condemning the practises that the employers were carrying out in the docks secretly they supported the shipping companies and as such he knew that they would never introduce legislation that could be seen as harming their friends the ship-owners.

Another obstacle that the dockworkers had to confront was the introduction of the National Insurance Act in 1911 this was to give unemployed workers a chance to claim 7 shillings a week unemployment pay. However dockworkers who had unsuccessfully sought work found themselves being refused any benefits as they were viewed under the poor law as being employed!! Heads they win and tails you lose again. This was just another example of how the Conservative's made life very uncomfortable for dockworkers and their families and this would continue right up to the late 1960s when decasualisation would finally be introduced.

Even as late as 1965 you could receive £11.00 for a week's attendance and although this was way below the amount that the Government deemed that you needed to live on you could not get any help from the state. Back in 1912 a dockworker who failed to secure any work could not present himself to the welfare board for some financial help as the law deemed that you had to be out of work for several consecutive days and had to prove that you had attempted to find work. This under the law debarred dockworkers from seeking help.

Then in 1919 Tillet and Bevan presented a joint claim to the employers for 16 shillings a day, increased overtime rates, better piece work rates, a payment for all men who had sought work and had been unsuccessful finally the joint trade unions wanted the immediate introduction of a registration scheme. All these claims had been submitted on the back of the Parliamentary enquiry under Shaw who had condemned the employers and had urged them to introduce better working conditions with the view to introducing a registration scheme at the earliest possible moment.

The employers found themselves on the back foot for once but in true Shipping companies tradition they settled down for a fight and their first ploy was to play for time. They dragged the talks on well into 1920 and after making a magnanimous gesture of agreeing with the unions that they would increase pay for those at work to 8 shillings per half a day in the major ports this was to be reduced to 7 shillings and sixpence in the smaller ports. They increased the overtime rates accordingly and the piece work rates were too increased. But on the question of payment for any dockworker who could not find a job and the most important claim for a registration they stubbornly dug their heels in but rather than reject it out of hand they along with the unions set up a joint working committee to look into these 2 points.

    The unions had no options other than to co-operate on this offer by the employers although it meant further delays to the main parts of the original claim. Of course the dock employers had absolutely no intention of conceding to the idea of paying men for not working and they knew that should a registration scheme be introduced the men would rightfully demand payment whether they were at work or not. All this was taking place against a backdrop of severe economic hardships; unemployment was running at 12% of the population with inflation running at anything from 15% up to a staggering 25%. Yet the dockworkers wages along with the majority of the working classes saw little change in their wages.

    Yes these were the roaring 20s if you had money the high life was out there for you however at the other end of the scale the misery continued in fact it had got worse as prices had increased making an already uphill struggle to survive almost impossible to feed your family. It was around this time that Bevin who was giving evidence to one of the many enquiries took in and presented before the committee a typical meal that a dockworkers family would eat in the evening. He placed the plate of food which was sparse and did not look very appetising on the table where the employers representatives were seated and stated "this is the sole meal that many of my members get to eat each day they are then expected to carry out the most arduous work in the most pitiful conditions" he then continued by challenging the employers if they could survive on these rations.

Mores the pity that present day trade union leaders never took a leaf out of Bevin's style of leadership. It was this and the evidence that Bevin had presented to the various committees that had won him the leadership of the new mighty union that had been formed by merging several unions into one giant union. This union was to be called the Transport & General Workers Union and it was created in 1922.

The plan being was that by creating a huge cross section of the different industries the workers could threaten untold trouble to both the employers and the Government thus getting their members the wages and the working conditions that they sought. However this may look mighty good on paper but in real life this was hardly ever used. In the case of the dockworkers this mighty union with a huge cross section of members it would work against them when the battle over containerisation was to take place some 40 years later.

It would be the mid-1920s that the real trouble would kick in unemployment began to rise at an alarming rate and once again many labourers who had lost their jobs began to try and get work on the docks. As the 1920s where coming to an end deflation took grip of the British economy, work in the docks began to peter out as demand for goods fell; the trade unions did everything in their power to protect their workers rates of pay and conditions. Given the wretched working conditions that existed that side of the trade unions actions could not have been too difficult.

Because of this and Winston Churchill's determination in pegging the pound against the U.S Dollar at the level it was prior to the First World War. It was sheer madness to attempt this as the country was already struggling to combat deflation brought about by some bad Government decisions but to peg the pound at $4.26 to one English pound. This again was Churchill at his worst as Chancellor of the Exchequer. History shows that this was not Great Britain's finest moment. What this did was to make an already serious crisis more critical. Companies began to lay workers of whilst other companies seized the moment and started reducing workers' wages.

The most famous example of this was the mine owners who reduced the miners pay by an astonishing 13% and as if that wasn't bad enough they also increased each shift by 1 hour. When the miners and their unions refused to accept these new working hours and new rates of pay the mine owners locked out 800,000 miners. This went on for 2 days and when the TUC realised that the mine owners where not for negotiating a general strike was called. Bevin who was a member of the T.U.Cs general council was against calling a general strike as he believed that the trade union movement needed more time before embarking on such a precarious campaign.

However much Bevin voiced his opposition against a general strike other members of the general council sympathised with the plight of the miners knowing that if the mine owners got away with this then most other employers would follow suit almost immediately. So on the 4th of May 1926 a general strike began. It soon become apparent that the T.U.C had entered this dispute with mixed feelings and that they were looking for a way out rather than seeking a meaningful solution that would protect both the miners and all other workers who would face the same fate as the miners.

Dockworkers were called out on strike from the outset along with transport workers and most key workers in British industries. Many others who had not been told to strike joined in and within a couple of days 1.7 million workers were out on strike in support of the miners. The Government had been prepared for such a showdown and had plans in place to try and keep the country fed and watered.

It was the middle classes and the students who nearly all were from very rich stock who thought it was a bit of fun to man the buses and do anything that might help break the strike. Food ships were unloaded under the protection of armed guards whilst the transport again being driven by strike breaking students or troops that would deliver the meat to the wholesale markets was accompanied by troops in armoured cars with machine guns at the ready. Given these conditions there was very little violence which was not surprising as any move to stop the strike breakers or the movement of the cargos that they had unloaded would have seen carnage in the shape of troops opening fire on demonstrators.

The Government likened the strike to the Russian revolution that had taken place some 7 years earlier. In the Government daily news sheet The British Gazette they called the strike leaders anarchists, revolutionaries or communist sympathisers. You paid your penny for the news sheet and you took your pick whilst Churchill put paid to the T.U.Cs response by stopping all the newsprint that was required to print their strike edition The British Worker. Even the King who usually remained impartial and silent on constituenial matters by stating to the Prime Minister "try and live on their wages before you judge them" when discussing the striking miners.

However the truth of the matter was that the General Council of the T.U.C had been holding secret talks daily with the Prime Minister and their heart was not in it and rather than find a satisfactory solution that would be acceptable to the miners all they were concerned with was trying to find a way of ending the dispute that they themselves had instigated. Despite all the propaganda and the efforts of the ruling classes to carry on strike breaking their efforts were merely token gestures because food was in short supply as were essential goods.

As the strike continued the strikers were becoming more and more agitated by the attitude of the T.U.C and some strikers decided that the softly softly approach was wrong and they began to engage in a more aggressive campaign. A group of railwayman derailed "The Flying Scotsman" this was a famous train that travelled between

London and Edinburgh. Also pickets at the docks began to become more aggressive towards the strike breakers. The few London buses that were on the streets now had to have either the police or soldier's on board protecting the driver and the conductor.

On the 7th of May the T.U.C met members of the cabinet and Sir Herbert Samuel and worked out a draft agreement for a settlement that would see an end to the general strike. However any optimism would be very short lived as the Miners Federation who represented all the entire pit owners dismissed the recommendations out of hand and refused point blank to enter any further negotiations. The general council had played their last card and all that was left for them to do now was to find a way of ending the dispute that was paralysing the nation. Bevin who had been against the strike from the beginning knew that the game was up and he also knew that when the general council threw in the towel not only would it be the defeat of all defeats but union membership and trade union participation would suffer as a result of it.

Then on May the 12th the leaders of the T.U.C once again visited the Prime Minister at 10 Downing Street to announce to him that they were calling of the strike. Thy sought assurances that all employers would re-engage all workers and not victimise strike leaders and activists to which the Prime Minister responded with that he had no jurisdiction over individual employers. So the T.U.C left with absolutely no concessions whatsoever. The strike was called off and many members who had actively participated in the strike found themselves blacklisted and without any chance of getting a job for many years.

The miners who had been betrayed by the T.U.C continued with their dispute and it was another 6 months before all the pits were back to work however once again the leaders and organisers of the strike found themselves blacklisted and unable to get any work. As for the few who had returned to work before the dispute was ended they had to endure a lifetime of hatred and bitterness towards them and their families. Such was the price of being a scab. Meanwhile back in the docks the strike had left many union members wondering if it was all worth it but Bevin once again led the unions charge towards obtaining a registration by this time using the recently introduced unemployment act whereby his members found little benefit from the scheme if they had found a day's work and then been unemployed for the rest of the week. The Government amended the scheme to cater for such cases and the scheme was now amended to include anyone who was unemployed for any three days in the last six days. Dockworkers seized on this and before long many of them did just 3 days work and signed on to obtain the insurance relief money.

Government after Government failed to get the shipowners and the stevedoring contractors to bring about an end to the casual system. The Government knew that the only solution to ending the abuse of the insurance act was to give the dockworkers some sort of registration scheme but the employers were having none of it. No matter how many times the Government changed the insurance act the problem of how to deal with dockworkers and their families in times of unemployment continued to dog whatever actions the Government took.

Committee after committee sat on the question of ending the casual system in the docks and time after time the employers resisted any changes. Every wage claim was accompanied by a demand to decasualize the industry. Every time the employers would offer to set up a committee to look into the matter. Bevin knew that the employers had absolutely no intentions of decasualising the docks and that by continually setting up so called committees they were buying time before they would turn down any committee's findings.

It wasn't just the employers who resisted introducing a registration scheme but Bevin found that even amongst his own members there was some opposition. This came generally from the favoured few who generally had a regular job on the call on system. This was when a foreman or a ship worker wanted men to work their ship and they usually hired men who they knew how to work that particular ship. Furthermore as they were regular and knew all about the workings of that particular job then the ship was unloaded faster. These men didn't want any changes as they thought it may threaten what they already had.

But, as always Bevin soldiered on, raising the question of decasualisation at every opportunity. Given the magnitude of the defeat that the working class movement had suffered it was now a question of treading water and regaining the men's confidence. It was Bevin again who tried to corner the employers by changing the claim for a registration scheme to a scheme whereby the employers along with the Government would pay the unemployed dockworkers out of a maintenance pool. He also put into the claim a demand that the employers create light duty jobs for the older dockworkers or those that had been too badly injured to enable them to do heavy duty work.

Bevin thought he had the employers and when asked by them to expand on the maintenance programme he told the employers that due to the vast area that the docks in London covered he would expect 5 or 6 clearing stations where men who had been unable to get work on the call would report to there to "prove attendance" and get their book stamped which would at the end of the week give the men who had proved attendance a fall back payment that would come from the maintenance pool. This pool would be funded by placing a small levy on the men who had found work or a levy on the tonnage that the men had handled.

This was Bevin's finest hour he had trapped the employers into discussing a scheme that was a registration in all but name. He also won admiration from all quarters on how he had presented the claim. Whilst the employers had smelt a rat they were slowly being forced into a corner and lo and behold the maintenance scheme was accepted in principle. The employers wanted an assurance that it would not lead to a full blown registration scheme. But Bevin was far to canny for them he merely answered this with his coupe da grace by asking the employers if they had a ship in one of the zones that had exhausted all their men then surely a telephone call to another zone who had a surplus of labour that day and the men could be despatched to a job that otherwise would have remained unmanned.

So the first scheme was born with any man reporting to the "box" would receive eight shillings for attending and he would have to report back at 1 p.m. to see if there was any fresh work available, if there wasn't his book would be duly stamped and he would be eligible for another eight shillings. However should the employers send a man to work his pay would be set against whatever the maintenance money he was entitled to. In short all he would receive if the man had proved attendance for 3 days and he was then sent to work for the rest of the week and his wages were in excess of £4 then the 3 days' pay he had accrued by proving attendance would be wiped out. You were guaranteed £4.00. This was a major breakthrough and the principle of Bevin's maintenance scheme was still in operation right up to 1967 but under a different name.

But the best was still yet to come. Bevin flushed with success in obtaining the maintenance scheme now went after the dock employers for a full registration that would see the end of the causal system that had dogged the industry since well before the 1889 strike. He had seen the employers hindering negotiation's by constantly referring the matter to a sub-committee or setting up another committee to look into the matter. Bevin was wise now to all these moves that the employers had used in an effort to blatantly shirk responsibilities of engaging the men on a permanent basis.

This was what nearly all other workers had and they just took it for granted that if you got a job then the employer took you on and the responsibility that came with employing people. Not so the dock employers- they had a very nice little scheme going whereby they used the labour to work their ships as and when they wanted men but when it came to providing them with the added protection of a regular wage and decent working conditions then the whole ball game changed their attitude was we are quite happy with what we have got and we don't need changes thank you very much!

The T & G W U under Bevin's leadership knew that they had a massive challenge on their plate in trying to secure a registration scheme that would bring about the decasualisation of the dock industry. Little did they know that it take would a world war in 1939 to get registered and an act of Parliament in 1946 to get a full registered scheme and a further 47 years wait before the industry was decasualised!!

What Bevin had legislated under the emergency war powers was to set up National Dock Labour Corporation who would grant the dockworkers a war time registration and it was the Corporation who allocated men to work but only to registered employers. Should there be no work then the men would receive unemployment pay that would come from the Governments National Insurance scheme and the employers who would pay a levy into the fund from working dockworkers. Taking into account that labour was in demand with a shortage of abled men due to the demands of the war there was not much unemployment.

Bevin The Dockers K.C

As the country began to slide into the recession (I don't refer to it as the great recession as there was nothing great about it) the docks as was always the case felt it first as demand for goods fell away and as a result ships had very little cargos and before long ships were laid up because of there was no cargos for them. The recession was world-wide and unemployment soared. Bevan knew that it was imperative for the dockworkers to obtain a registration. Talks began in earnest about bringing an end to the longest running saga that any industry had ever seen. Given the sheer scale of the unemployed dockworkers the employers were more determined than ever that they should not pay unemployment pay on a regular basis or even pay the men some holiday pay.

So began what must go down in history as the longest negotiations ever. Not taking into account the previous years where the employers put off and stalled talks the Dockworkers unions made it abundantly clear that they wanted to enter earnest talks with a view of introducing the end of a system that would hold pride of place in one of Dickens novels.

Bevin knew that it had taken 7 years of talks before the maintenance programme had been accepted by the ship-owners and the stevedoring contractors so he dug in knowing that they would resist claims for a full registration. Over the course of the next 9 years the Government would hold enquiries, Royal Commissions into the question of decasualisation. Whilst the newly set up National Joint Council for the port transport industry met on numerous occasions in trying to bring about a solution.

    Every time the employers looked like they might be ready to settle and give way to the union's demands when they would request that another committee look into a small matter that they claimed was troubling them. They were past masters at stalling the talks. The talks went on for 7 years before the employers finally run out of ideas in putting of the trade unions and they now had the Government on their backs urging them to enter serious talks with a view to bringing to an end of the casual system. Then in 1937 the trade unions submitted a wage claim with the main plank of the claim being that the unemployed dockworkers receive a large increase in the maintenance pay, because the employers had been railroaded into this scheme they had continually refused to increase the pay for dockworkers that were unemployed.

    The employers knew that the game was up and they even had the audacity to announce to the unions that "they" wanted to introduce a registration scheme and invited the unions to join with them in holding talks so as a fair scheme could be introduced. They emphasised that such a scheme must be fair to all parties and a registration scheme should be phased in gradually so as the costs could be absorbed rather than a scheme that would see their costs rocket.

Only these people could have the effrontery to state this after decades of treating their labour force as if they were animals. The call on system had not changed since the back end of the nineteenth century. Government enquiries and Royal Commission's along with the newspapers of all political persuasions had likened the call on system to a cattle market auction. Yet they still persisted with it and they still recruited many hundreds of men over and above the required labour force strength so as when they were busy they had all the labour that they needed. But what was really the truth was that in all probability for 9 or 10 months in a year the surplus labour had absolutely no chance of finding work.

Any employer who could have the luxury of employing extra labour to cover them for periods when they were busy would soon go bust as the expense of carrying a surplus labour force when the slack times arrive would lead to serious financial problems. Not so with the dock employers they didn't care that there could be 3 or 4 thousand extra men over what was normally need all they had to do was to pay these men the fall-back maintenance pay which had become pitifully low and even then they received the lion's share of the cost from the Governments welfare unemployment scheme. Added to this there was no holiday pay in place for the dockworkers and as for the working conditions their attitude was if you don't like it we will soon get someone else to do the job.

The employers finally entered into serious talks with the aim of giving every British dockworker a registration, but they then delivered a broadside. Whilst accepting the principle of the registration scheme they could not have the maintenance scheme incorporated into it! The unions could hardly believe what they had just heard yet again they wanted a regular labour force but when it came to paying the men their attendance pay the employers wanted out and that the Governments welfare scheme should pick up the bill.

Right through the 30s Governments tried to tackle the problem of forcing the employers to accept decasualisation. In 1934 when reforming the Unemployment Insurance Act they even caved in and offered the employers in the docks some financial assistance in paying the men who had no work. Again there was no response from the employers and as such that effort just tamely drifted into the sunset with no results.

Then in 1937 the unions in their annual wage claim submitted a claim that in view of the high unemployment in the docks which put their members as paid up members of the poverty club that the wages should be dramatically increased for those men who had secured a job. This would enable the men to save a few bob for when they were out of work. Once again the employers panicked at the thought of increased costs citing that it would drive work away.

What they really meant was that any wage increase would come out of the huge profits that stevedoring contractors were making. In some cases smaller stevedoring contractors could agree with a shipping company to unload their ship, engage the men required, borrow or "obtain" the necessary equipment needed to unload the ship and upon completion they never had to bother to tender for another job for about a year. In short they earned enough money from 1 job to keep them in clover for the next 12 months. The same cannot be said of the dockworkers they engaged to carry out their operations.

Once again the employers tied to wriggle out of the corner by increasing the pay by the mighty amount of one shilling a day. But, they included a rider that they now wanted to introduce a new scheme that would include giving the men a registration. The unions accepted the shilling and with both hands they grabbed the employer's offer of talks leading to changing the system.

These talks continued right into 1939 with a couple of serious sticking points the first being the unemployment pay, again the employers wanted the Governments Insurance Act to pick up the bill and then probably what would be the biggest stumbling block was the question of the size of the labour force. The Government quite rightly pointed out that if they were to consider assisting in paying the wages of the unemployed dockworkers then the register or the strength of the labour force should not have thousands of men that were generally over and above what the employers generally required.

Unions could not bring themselves to getting rid of men to satisfy the Government in reducing the size of the registers. However the Minister responsible for overseeing unemployment pay (The Unemployment Insurance Act) stated that the cost would be astronomical and as such the Government could not accept responsibility. The employers responded by claiming that at best the cost would "only "be £1,250.000 which would represent almost 80 million pound today. Talks dragged on and on and with the declaration of war with Germany anything else other than war measures was quickly overlooked. However a new twist would come to the rescue of all dockworkers.

Churchill had now become Prime Minister and he saw in Ernie Bevin a giant of a man who given his standing in the trade union movement. He approached him with the view of making him Minister of Labour. As Bevin was not an M.P, he had contested a couple of seats in the past, a quickly arranged seat was found. He was elected unopposed for the Wandsworth East seat. Bevin knew that this was his moment to use his new position to get the dockworkers a registration. Something that his union had strived for since its formation and had never got near achieving its goal. Now with war time measures in place he as Minister of Labour had powers that no employer, large or small, could argue with.

Bevin had now obtained powers that allowed him to control huge areas of Britain's workforce under the wartime powers granted to him by Parliament. He and Churchill knew that to keep feeding Britain the docks had to be kept working this gave Bevin the opportunity that he had tried unsuccessfully for years a registration scheme for the dockworkers.

What Bevin legislated was that all dockworkers be registered and this was a compulsory order as was the order that only registered employers would be allowed to engage labour to load and unload ships. Men could be transferred between ports depending on wherever the need for labour was the greatest. Historians are split as to whether the scheme was a success some state that it was a stroke of sheer brilliance while others state that the scheme was badly managed and led to huge delays in unloading vital cargos.

Probably Bevin is best remembered for his Bevin Boys programme where he overcome the acute shortage of miners to work the coal mines by conscripting thousands of boys who had been called up. They had to work the mines and keep the coal output up so as the British power stations could remain open and as such supply the nation with power. Coal was used to power the power stations. But to dockworkers Bevin would always be remembered as the person who brought the dock employers into line by introducing a register that gave war time dockworkers some form of security.

Despite all this dockworkers unloading ships faced danger in the form of Hitler's Luftwaffe trying to bomb the docks and the added perils of unloading and loading explosives that were needed for making bombs and mines. Docks were often damaged but in the main the German Air force generally missed the docks with their bombs and it was the surrounding areas that took the brunt of the bombing. The East End of London took a terrible pounding from the bombing that was aimed at destroying the docks with the lock gates that ships used to enter the docks being the main target. But it appeared that the German pilots were way of beam and in the main the docks managed to work on.

Bevin knew that once a scheme of a limited registration had been introduced the employers would not be able to return to the bad old ways. The scheme in fact was administrated by the Government so technically the dockworkers had become civil servants overnight! He had put into place The National Dock Labour Corporation to administer the scheme with equal numbers of trade union representatives and dock employers on a board who would be responsible for the running of their particular docks.

Because many of the original dockworkers had gone to fight the war it was not practicable to award the men charged with unloading and loading the ships with a full registration because when the war was over all men had the right to pick up their former jobs. What the war time scheme proved was that a registration scheme was workable in the docks contrary to what the employers had been banging on for years that a registration scheme and decasualisation of the industry would push costs to level that the industry could not sustain.

In 1944 as the tide was turning in the war Bevin told all parties in the docks to begin to prepare to draw up a scheme that could supersede the war time measures adding that each side should report their progress and their fears to him. Low and behold the employers submitted a set of proposals that started with the theme that whilst they shared the views that everyone expressed that the industry should not return to the bad old days they did however express their concerns some of which pointed to the facts that a jointly run industry was unworkable, they proposed that each port should be run by a committee that consisted of just employers representatives.

Once again the employers were using the tricks that they had used for decades in stalling talks and when the war finally ended no or at best very little progress had been made with the unions demanding that the new scheme should be run by joint committees made up from both trade union representatives and employer's.

Whilst the employers said that wages should be spread over a 4 week period with the men being guaranteed to earn £16 over that period, the unions stated that they wanted a minimum of £4 each week regardless of what a man may have earned the previous week and so it went on with talks dragging on and getting bogged down. This was exactly what the employers wanted and they were past masters at it.

But the dockworkers were fed up with the never ending delaying tactics that the employers were using which normally meant that the workers ended up with very little, if they were lucky. More often than not they got nothing. The tactic being that by delaying any claim for a prolonged period usually meant that the original claim that had been submitted accompanied by plenty of fire and passion would dwindle in time giving the employers the breathing space they required.

Such was the hardships faced by the overwhelmingly number of people after the war and it was generally accepted that the dockworkers suffered even greater hardships that it was not surprising that many of them had to resort to rather unconventional methods to get by. One schoolboy aged thirteen who had a job in a dockside café had called Ma Morgan's where he used to help out clearing the tables and taking the men's food to the table. If he knew them well or it was a family member he would slip a two bob bit (10p in today's language) into the bacon roll or sandwich and they would give him a shilling out of their ill-gotten gains! He would always take his days "booty" home and give it to his mother. He should have been on the apprentice!!

But as Bevin had held down important posts in both the war time coalition Government and then the interim coalition Government he knew the time had come to relinquish the post of general secretary of the T & G Enter Arthur Deakin. If Arthur Deakin had devoted a quarter of the time to his members instead of going on a crusade to root out "so-called reds" then perhaps the dockworkers would have enjoyed a better standard of living. He was Britain's answer to Senator Joe McCarthy the American politician who destroyed innocent people's livelihoods by their association with anyone who was thought to be a red. Deakin must have modelled his life on McCarthy's war on anyone who dares to question Government policy. What was even stranger was the fact that in the 1940s and the 1950s if you never had the support of the Catholic Church and the Communist party, then you never got a paid officials job with the T & G.

Dockworkers had not had a rise in their basic pay since 1922. It had remained fixed at 16 Shillings a day and any attempt however feeble by the unions to get it increased was fiercely opposed by the employers. The string of events that took place in 1945 really stretches the imagination. Firstly the supreme policy making body for the docks was the national delegates conference. There were 2 delegates from each port in the country. They passed a 6 point charter that become known as the dockers charter this conference was never known for its militancy as you could have 2 delegates from a tiny port that may employ 40 or 50 men whilst you had the same representation from the major ports who may represent 10 or 15 thousand men!   The Dockers Charter that was adopted as union policy was;-

    1/ An immediate rise in the basic wage from 16 Shillings to 25 Shillings.

    2/ Every dockworker to receive 2 weeks holiday with pay.

    3/ All dockworkers to receive the basic pay for public holidays.

    4/ An allowance scheme to be set up for the elderly and the infirm so as they might be able to retire once they could not carry out the strenuous requirements of dock work.

    5/ The working week be reduced from 44 hours to 40 hours.

    6/ The setting up of medical centres and welfare offices in every dock.

    These points were overwhelmingly accepted and the ink wasn't dry on the set of proposals when John Donovan the national docks secretary was expressing concerns that the "so called Docker's charter" was a communist and Trotskyist conspiracy! So in theory the Docker's chances had been dammed before they had even got off the ground. Not by the employers but by the very people who were supposed to represent the best interests of their members. Donovan along with other T & G paid officials had regular wage rises.

What happened next was that sporadic strikes flared up and in London a work to rule started which saw output drop alarmingly. All these actions were prompted by unofficial strike committees who given the absence in leadership from the official unions the men turned "to people they could trust". The ship-owners seized on the Luke warm attitude that had been showed by the leaders of the T & G by refusing to enter any talks whatsoever in connection to increasing the basic pay whilst the men were on strike. This further inflamed an already volatile situation and in ports that were not known for their militancy strike committees were elected at dock gate meetings. Before long forty thousand men were involved in various forms of industrial actions.

The newly elected Labour Government issued plea after plea to dockworkers to return to normal working because the war had left the country in a dire economic situation and the cry of the day was "export or die". Also despite several attempts by the strike leaders from the various ports to meet with Ministers met with no success at all as the Government did not want to upset the official union leadership.

Churchill had not hesitated to use the troops in

London's Surrey Commercial Docks to unload timber stating that the exports could not be held up by striking dockworkers. But that was before Labour had won the 1945 election with an astonishing victory that saw them with a majority of 145 seats.

So the new Labour Government was faced with a head on collision not with the trade unions but groups of men who they and the trade unions had no control over. Arthur Deakin waded in to the affray but announcing at a press conference the these strikes was the work of the communist revolutionary party and quickly added that he was not referring to the communist party who while supporting the dockworkers claims for better wages they disassociated themselves from any form of strike action that might harm a Labour Government.

Once again after being prompted by the Government the national joint council met to discuss the problem that was stopping over 200 ships from being worked. Once again the employers attacked the unions for not keeping their members under control and refused point blank to enter any talks whilst the men were engaged in industrial actions. Now if you can work that strategy out then you could qualify for a degree in industrial relations!

So the unions went on the offensive and issued leaflets and started calling mass meetings Not to discuss why the men were on strike or why these men had not seen their basic wage increased for the last 20 odd years but to tell them that they should go back to work and allow the machinery to handle any outstanding wage problems!

Deakin knew that the strike was at its strongest in

Liverpool and if the union could get Liverpool back to work then the strike would collapse and he duly despatched all his senior docks officers along with the 3 local M.Ps for Liverpool to meet with the strike committee in secret. What they proposed was that if they called the strike off then within a few weeks the basic wage would be increased. The M.P s witnessed this offer and so the Liverpool strike committee decided to give the union one last chance. They recommended to their men that they should return to work and they would reconvene the meeting in a few weeks' time to see whether the wages had been increased.

But the T & G had a nagging doubt word had reached them that in Liverpool and some of the other Northern ports that the men were considering forming a breakaway union. Now this is what the existing unions don't want to hear, despite their inability to secure a decent wage for their members and improve the terrible working conditions in the docks they did not want to lose membership. So for a while it was all change in their attitude towards the men. With Liverpool returning to work the other ports all gradually drifted back. The union knew that the key to breaking the strike was Liverpool and some 6 weeks later the unions reported that they had achieved a rise in the basic wage as promised.

The rise as the union put it was nowhere near what the original claim had been in fact all that the unions had secured from the employers was an increase of three shillings a day. But the unions knew that the men's resolve had been broken with the long drawn out dispute and as such it was accepted. As for the remaining points in the

Docker's charter well they had sunk without a trace.

There was still no sign of dockworkers receiving paid holidays and as for retirement well that was like a mirage in the desert- you can see it but it's not there. So the old boys either ended up in the workhouse or they carried on working until they died. But the men were thoroughly disgusted with what the trade unions had accepted and the dye was cast for the next decade or so with the emergence of the unofficial committees in the major ports. The men knew that they could trust these men unlike the trade unions who had treated the men with contempt year after year. The men now looked to the unofficial committees to take forward any grievance's that might pop up.

With the Labour Government now firmly in place with the whopping majority that they had Bevin now got what he had been striving for. Although he was not Minister of Labour the cabinet looked to him to draw up the white paper that would see the introduction of the National Dock Labour Scheme and that would give all dockworkers the registration that they had sought for so long. With this would come holiday pay, unemployment pay paid for by your employers and a whole host of things that the unions had attempted to bring in over the previous twenty odd years. The Minister of Labour was George Isaacs and it would be he who would present the bill to Parliament but anyone who was anyone knew that Bevin was the architect of the whole thing.

Once the paper was put in front of Parliament the Conservative's didn't know how to oppose a bill that a parties had said was long overdue and that the working conditions in the docks were an embarrassment to the country as a whole. But they did give it their best shot in trying to stall the bills progress but with a majority of over a hundred and forty if the Government had said that Nottingham was in Scotland then they could have got away with it!

As sure as small acorns grow into huge oaks the employers tried everything that they could to either halt the bills progress or receive very favourable terms when it came to paying the dockworkers that had no work. The Government become tired of listening to the employers tales of woe and instructed all parties that the war time measures should be kept in place as and from February 14th 1946 until the Government had time to get its bill through Parliament which would see all dockworkers become registered.

You have to take your hat off to the ship-owners and the stevedoring contractors who despite knowing that this Labour Government could do whatever they liked given their majority in the house. Despite this they objected, they failed to respond when the Minister asked interested parties for their observations leaving the Government to appoint Sir John Forster K.C to hold an enquiry into the differences that both parties had, he was then to report back with his recommendations.

Sir John Forester's report was to be the framework for the bill to be published soon afterwards. The Minister invited all parties to take the opportunity to object to any part of the report and when both the employers and the unions both submitted their concerns the Minister then appointed John Cameron as an independent arbitrator to hear all objections and advise the Minster of his decision on all the points that had been objected to. On the question of pay the Minister appointed yet another person to chair a committee he was an academic named Sir Hector Hetherington. He again listened to all the evidence that both parties put forward and recommended to the Minister that any man not finding work should receive 5 shillings for that period. He also recommended that anyone who had not secured work that week should be paid the fall back guarantee of four pounds seven shillings and sixpence per week, this was for attending the call on and then the dock labour office twice a day plus Saturday morning.

Probably in sheer desperation and never realising what a can of worms they had opened the Government published a bill that would bring the dock labour force under an act of Parliament. The Newly set up National Joint Council for the port transport industry would monitor wages and working conditions and they agreed that the fall back guarantee should be four pounds eight shillings per week this was an extra sixpence per week over and above what the last committee had recommended. Another tanner the docks history seems to be littered around the famous "Tanner"!

The bill was to be the Dock Workers (Regulation of Employment) Order 1947. Contained in it was the setting up of local dock labour boards which would be made up with employers and trade union representation and they would be responsible to see that the act was being carried out correctly, amongst they duties local boards also found themselves responsible for discipline that ranged from a suspension without pay up to summary dismissal. The question on the size of the register was for the National Dock Labour Boards committee to have the final say after recommendations from the local dock labour boards. The national board also was responsible for such things such as holiday pay. The costs that these boards incurred by paying unemployment and holiday pay would be recouped via a levy that was fixed at 15% on every registered dockworkers gross daily earnings. The levy fluctuated depending on the local ports financial needs.

On the question of recruitment the employers made it quite clear that much of the work that is undertaken was seasonal and as such agreement was reached that local boards could recruit labour under seasonal registers scheme. Any man who was recruited under this scheme had to be made aware that his services could end with an agreed period of notice. These were called limited men.

This scheme was gradually dispensed with and all recruitment was directly into the main register with the man getting a full registration. Recruitment was to be 50% trade union nominations and the same for the employers over the years the trade union usually took a much greater percentage of all recruitments. The trade union nominations came from fathers whose sons wanted to work in the dock industry.

So on the 28th June 1947 the act was put into practise in every registered port in Britain. It wasn't utopia by a long way for the dockworkers but given how they had been treated in the past it was a major milestone. Over the years they attempted to address some of the anomalies that the act had overlooked or had not been able to include because of the fear of an employer's backlash. However it would be 8 years before any changes were made to the scheme. On introducing the scheme there were 74,000 men who had become registered this was a reduction of some 11,000 men from the pre-war figure.

One of the new aspects of the scheme was the right for men to be disciplined by the local dock labour board if they were in contravention of their contract; they also had the right to appeal against any penalties that the board may have handed out. Arthur Deakin was getting very concerned that the unofficial committee's that had sprung up and down the country were getting far too powerful and he was on the warpath to rid the docks of the men who were on these committees.

Most of these leaders were dockworkers who also belonged to the communist party. Deakin was convinced that they were out to smash British democracy and that they were using Britain's docks to help follow the revolution that Russia had seen in 1917.

But before we view Arthur's exploits we must understand what led him to embark on his crusade. The new scheme was still in its infancy and whilst the employers secretly despised everything that the scheme offered the men they were determined to sabotage it at every possible opportunity that they could. The men were getting fed up with the local dock labour boards position of punishment. Under the new scheme men who misbehaved, were caught stealing or were in breach of the scheme would be reported by the employer to the local board who would hand out a suspension.

The man then had the right of appeal under the scheme. However more and more men were getting punished and when it came to their appeals being heard hardly anyone was ever successful. This was a bitter pill for the men to swallow as the committee that heard the appeals was made up with 2 trade union officials and 2 employers with an independent chairman. The whole thing was to kick off in a big way, and Arthur Deakin didn't like the fact that his members were challenging the roles that certain trade union officials were playing. The men expected a little more support.

A typical example of how the unions treated their members came to the surface when some men were told to load 100 tons of Zinc Oxide onto a ship. When all of the men's skin turned blue they checked out the dangers of the cargo at a local library which showed that the substance fell into the "poisonous" category and that it should not be inhaled or come into contact with your skin. That was enough for the gang to ask for an additional award for working this cargo.

Under the new scheme if the men thought that the piece work rate was insufficient then they could request a viewing committee who would look at the job and decide if it warranted an extra payment. The piece work rate for this particular job was 3 shillings and 4pence per ton and the men asked that this be increased to 5 shillings per ton. The viewing committee turned the request down, stating that the existing rate covered that job correctly.

    The men refused to accept that they had been given a fair hearing and refused to work the remaining 75 tons and the ship duly sailed with only 25 tons of the 100 tons having been discharged. The employers had tried to get another gang to do the job who claimed that as the job was in dispute they would not work it. The original gang were duly reported to the local dock board and that would normally be that. But for some unknown reason the ship returned to the Regents Canal and the same men were instructed to finish off loading the remaining 75 tons of Zinc Oxide.

    The unions sent in the big guns and agreed that a new viewing committee should inspect the job, which they did and they made no award whatsoever which not surprisingly led to the men refusing to work it at that rate. The shipping company now reported the men to the local board for the third time.

    The local board met the very next day and found the men to be in breach of the agreement. The employers wanted the men sacked on the spot, but the board's findings were that the men should be suspended for 7 days and that should any of the men be unemployed for the next 3 months they would not receive any unemployment pay. The men were outraged at this decision and although they had a further right to appeal the touch paper had been lit. It was a union delegate who started the strike off firstly by getting the whole of the Regents Canal men out on strike and then going around to the other docks in seeking support.

The T & G.W.U paid officials were hurried into action to get the men back to work. This was typical of the union that rather than try and seek a settlement with the employers and then get the men to accept it they just instructed the men to return to work and in doing this they would rubbish the strike leaders.

The London Dock Labour Board manager never helped matters when he said that the punishment metered out to the men was not only justified but should serve as a warning to any other men who were considering similar actions. The Regent Canal and the London Docks had shop stewards a luxury that the rest of London's dockworkers would have to wait another 25 years before they were given the right to elect shop stewards at your place of work.

But before long the strike was spreading throughout London and before long an unofficial committee was set up and as it consisted of working dockworkers who understood and shared the same problems as the men it was more readily accepted by the men. The trade union officials who were often bogged down by red tape, and a hard and fast constitution, that would mean that the men's problems could take months before they could be dealt with.

The shop stewards and the unofficial committees on the other hand not only shared any problems that could crop up at work but they could convene a meeting almost immediately to discuss the problem. This would put them at loggerheads with the trade unions for years to come.

What bedevilled the trade unions (especially the T & G) was that if the men had a grievance then they had to attend their union branch meeting and get it accepted. Then after a few weeks another committee that was made up of branch delegates would sit and consider it. Should it pass that hurdle it would be sent to the next committee the Docks Group Committee who again would consider it and if it was a matter that could affect the national agreement then they would send it to the national docks group committee. This exercise could easily take 3 or 4 months.

But the unofficial committees had no negotiating rights at all and as would be the case for decades to come any dispute that the men entered into would have to be settled by the official trade union committees. The trade unions called a meeting in London's Victoria Park with a view to getting all the men on strike back to work. Their incompetence only served to see the strike grow larger the next day! In fact when the tally clerks threw their lot in with the strikers, that was game, set and match. The Port of London had ground to a complete halt.

The Government now intervened by stating if the stoppage was not completely ended then they would have no alternative other than to begin to unload food ships to keep the nation fed. The T & G hurriedly called meetings to get the men back to work they drew up a leaflet that was to be issued stating how wrong the men were and they also proposed calling a meeting at London's Royal Albert Hall!

The Governments emergency powers committee also examined the role of certain members of the strike committee and came up with the view that as some of the members were communists there might be a conspiracy to overthrow an elected Government. Now I ask you had the original viewing committee offered the men a couple of shillings to load the Zinc Oxide then all of this could easily have never taken place. This was a classic example of how the unions had become out of touch with their members and how arrogant the employers were with their attitude towards the labour force.

Events had now grown to alarming proportions and the strike committee called another meeting at Victoria Park to clash with Deakins debut at the Royal Albert Hall. The strike committee stated that the men could choose who best represented their views. However Deakin agreed to hold a secret meeting with a small delegation from the strike committee and he expressed his fears that the strike was not only damaging the British economy but certain elements were using it to bring down the Labour Government. A sure fire way of attempting to bring about a settlement!

Deakins Albert Hall appearance turned out to be a personal disaster perhaps it was first night nerves! Only 2,000 turned up to hear him while over at Victoria Park an estimated 11,000 men heard the strike leaders promise that if a settlement wasn't forthcoming they would travel to other ports to get them to join the strike. Also there was talk of forming a breakaway union for the first time. The whole of the negotiating machinery was now thrown at the striking dockworkers which culminated in the men going back to work when dismissal notices for being in breach of the scheme were being sent out, this was not before the troops had been brought in to unload perishable foodstuffs. The resentment of how the men had been blackmailed into returning to work would remain in the minds of many.

Not only had the unions failed to get a settlement that would have seen the men return to work with a little honour but the whole dispute had been overshadowed by accusations of a communist conspiracy. Deakin took this up to avenge the shame and embarrassment that he had endured during the strike. Lurking ominously in the background was a piece of war time legislation that stopped people from urging others to strike, although never enacted this piece of legislation could lead to people being charged at the highest level on the charge of conspiracy to strike. The Labour Government had assured everyone that they would repel this as soon as they took office. They later confessed that they had forgotten about it!

Apart from the odd flare up here and there major strikes were becoming a thing of the past but the dockworkers still very suspicious of the trade union officials still listened to the unofficial leaders who not only shared their hardships and done the same hard work but most importantly they spoke their language.

Despite the introduction of the dock labour scheme working conditions had hardly changed. You still had to endure the indignantly of the call on twice a day. Nothing really had changed here at all. Sometimes you could have a good few thousand men going on the call to try and secure one of a hundred jobs or so. Sometimes with the pushing and shoving in an attempt to catch the foreman's eye so as he would give you a job there were fights and tempers reached boiling points more often than not. Good friends would fight to get the job and any comradeship that existed went right out of the window when it came to getting a job. This could have been the difference between feeding your family and totally going without.

Working conditions too had not altered with piece work being in evidence at every job; this meant that in order to reach your daily goal all forms of safety would be ignored which in turn led to a massive amount of industrial accidents. Many of these accidents would leave the injured dockworker with injuries that would prevent him from being able to return to carry out his former job. Perhaps these were the fortunate ones as many dockworkers lost their lives through accidents at work. To compound it all if a man was involved in an accident he received no sick pay at all which normally meant that the man would have to return to work long before his injuries had cleared up, this also applied to men who had been struck down with illness they too would be forced to return to work before their bodies had a chance of recovering from whatever illness had forced them to be absent from work.

The Witch-hunts

The recent events that had seen the trade unions lose any confidence that the men had held. However what happened as a result of this would see more strife heaped upon an already beleaguered labour force in the early 1950s.Deakin along with the Government were determined to get the strike leaders who they saw as communist agitators.

The Government put M.I.5 onto the case and all the strike leaders in Liverpool and London were put under close scrutiny. Meanwhile not to be outdone Deakin sent instructions that all these men and their supporters were to be "branched" with a view to removing there trade union membership. To be branched by the trade union is like being prosecuted but instead of facing a magistrate you are judged by union delegates, you can be branched for a whole host of things but the one that you usually found yourself being charged with was the rule where you are committing untrade union like activities. This rule is in most trade union rule books and covers a whole host of events.

In London alone over two hundred men were brought before the trade union committees and even the local Dock Labour Board got in on the act by disciplining certain strike leaders. What had led all parties to take this drastic action? It was events in 1949 when the Canadian seamen were in dispute with their employers on the East Coast of Canada. Ships that had been placed in dispute had been manned with so-called black leg labour. The Canadian seamen's union made a request to all British dockers not to work any of the ships that had been caught up in the dispute. In short the Canadian seamen's union were caught up in their own inter union dispute in Canada where an anti-communist union made up primarily of French Canadian seamen had struck a deal with the ship-owners who in turn sacked the existing seamen with whom they had an agreement.

Ships that had already set sail from Canada with crews from the union that was in dispute with the shipping companies contacted the various port committees as soon as they docked with a plea not to unload the cargos. The T & G who were part of the International Transport Federation, a group of influential trade unions who had come together in the name of international solidarity.

The T & G could not boast solidarity in this country yet alone worldwide solidarity. But the employers who smelt trouble and as such as soon as the disputed ships docked in Bristol, Liverpool and London they were left idle. No attempt was made to put dockworkers on these ships to begin discharging them.

However the T & G received a get out of jail card by the way of the International Transport Federation who stated that these ships were not in dispute as the trouble in Canada was directly a result of an inter union dispute. The employers in Bristol directed labour to the Seaboard Queen the ship that was being placed in dispute by the crew. The Bristol dockworkers refused to work the ship and when the men were put of pay a strike began in the port of Bristol.

The Labour Government was getting fed up with these disputes in the docks that were having a bad effect on both our exports and the ability of the Government to be able to feed the nation albeit a meagre amount of food each week by the way of ration book coupons. Southampton and Leith both saw Canadian ships that were affected by the seamen's dispute arrive and unlike the Bristol dock labour board no attempt was made to send men to work these ships. With Bristol practically at a standstill the Government deployed 1,200 troops to work strike bound ships. The strike leaders at Bristol came up with a solution that would solve the dispute they asked that the troops unload the Canadian ship so as the rest of the port could then get back to normal working.

The Ministers who were in charge of deploying the troops refused this request and put the troops to work on other ships. The reason given for this was that the dock labour scheme had sent men to work a ship who had then refused to carry out their obligations as laid out in the new scheme. When a ship that had been diverted from Bristol to

Liverpool berthed the dockworkers there refused to work it stating that it was a disputed ship. The local dock labour board duly allocated men to work the ship and when they refused to accept the job the rest of the men were not sent to work.

    Gradually the strike had now built up in Liverpool with some ten thousand men now out on strike. There was no doubt in the Governments mind and the unions that this whole affair was a communist conspiracy. The Government now repeated their actions that had an effect in ending the previous stoppage by appealing to the men through a radio broadcast. It appeared to work for 2 days later the dockworkers of Bristol voted to return to work and to work the Canadian ship that had been the centre of the trouble. There had been 2 Canadian ships berthed in London for 6 weeks and to avert any trouble no labour had been sent to work the ships. But, given the men's decision in Bristol the London Dock Labour Board met with a view to allocate dockworkers to these 2 ships. Donovan had gone as national docks secretary with his post being taken up By Arthur Bird who when the chips were down ducked the meeting, leaving Dickie Barret the general secretary of the National Amalgamated Stevedores & Dockers more commonly known in the docks as the blue union to face the music alone. He had already instructed his members not to work these ships and when the London Board meeting after a request from the Minister for Labour decided that under the terms of the dock labour scheme these ships should be worked.

    But Barret had to throw the towel in as behind the

scenes threats had been made that the Government would not hesitate to prosecute Barret and his union under an old act of Parliament the 1305 act which was a war time act preventing anyone from inciting men to strike. As the blue union was only a small union compared to the size and might of the T & G they had no option other than to climb down. But then the T & G members refused to work the ships and before long work had ceased completely in the Royal Group of docks and the ship in the Surrey Commercial docks. Many other dockworkers in the West India & Millwall docks joined in the strike.

    The threats that the Government were making to prosecute under a war time Act of Parliament was no idle threat and they now turned their attention to the unofficial leaders of the strikes that had plagued the port of London. Nothing however was being done about the appalling wages and working conditions that was still widely commonplace in the dock industry. If the unions had righted these appalling working conditions then there would have been no need for an unofficial committee.

    It never took long before the whole thing kicked off in London despite Dickie Barret's objections, men in both the Surrey docks and the Royal docks were ordered to work the 2 Canadian ships on June 21st. Within a week the whole of the Royals and the Surrey docks were out on strike. The unofficial committee were claiming that it was a lock out as the dockworkers were perfectly willing to work every other ship in the docks. Men from the West India and Millwall docks now joined in the strike.

    The leadership of the T & G were absolutely furious

and were determined to root out the unofficial leaders but in the meantime some 15 thousand men were back out on strike. The men had the employers, the T &G.W.U union and the Government against them also the press were in a frenzy over the communist leaders of the strike. Not much hope given the batting order against you.

Once again troops were drafted into the docks to ensure that the nation's food cupboards were kept stocked up. The total number of troops used increased as each day of the strike went on in the end there were some ten thousand soldiers working ships in the strike hit docks. But then the London Dock Labour Board started to issue dismissal notices under the terms of the scheme. Along with employers who had a regular work force of men who enjoyed regular work, and normally a better standard of living threatening to return them to the labour pool things began to take a different twist. .

So the men returned to work after five weeks on strike the unions could not understand why the men still held the unofficial leaders with the same high regard. Deakin was now spitting blood and he told his docks group committee that he wanted these men out of the union at any cost.

What happened next is almost beyond belief. It is most probably the Transport & General Workers Unions most shameful period in the unions long history. Under Deakins leadership and his orders to all of his paid officers and the most senior delegates the order was given to kick out the communists from the union. This as Deakin knew would also lead to these men losing their livelihoods as it was taken for granted by the men in the docks that "no union card meant no work". If a man could not produce an up to date union card then he was not engaged by the ganger on the call. The union card was the Holy Grail to the dockers no matter how hard up a man might have been he always found the money to pay his union dues.

So many of the unofficial committee members found themselves being hauled up before trade union committees to face a grilling on why they had incited men to strike which was in direct opposition to the official trade union policy. As if this wasn't bad enough men who actively had supported the unofficial committee found themselves being hauled up in front of the same committees. What Deakin had overlooked was the fact that many of these committee members were friends of the people that were being charged.

The union delegates found it very hard to find the men guilty of any charges that had been brought against them as they knew that if the accused men were found guilty on just one minor charge then that man's livelihood was under threat.

Still unperturbed by this Deakin then changed his attack by getting the local dock labour board to issue disciplinary procedures against the most senior members of the unofficial committee members. Again this could lead to the men being dismissed if the charges were proven and this time there would be no mates or friends on the committees that heard the charges. Indeed the disciplinary committee was made up of 2 employers and 2 senior trade union officials with an independent chairman.

But yet again the threat of removing the unofficial leaders from the dock labour scheme had not materialised in fact when one of the employers representatives on the dock labour board asked Harry Constable if he knew that he was breaking the law in inciting men to strike he replied by asking the employer if he was aware that swimming in the dock was forbidden and as such anyone swimming in the dock would be breaking the law. Constable then asked the employer what he would do if he saw a man drowning. If he jumped in to save the man this would be breaking the law!

Not that anyone would ever want to swim in the docks with the water so filthy and polluted that anyone just falling into the water had to go to the hospital to be pumped out! So despite the dock labour boards valiant attempt to rid the industry of its unofficial leaders not much ever came of their actions. Perhaps it was the fact that the employers knew that if the men were dismissed then an all-out strike was a distinct possibility even without the leaders. This was not how Arthur Deakin and the Government had planned the script.

Yet again Deakin had spent so much time and effort in trying to remove the men who were showing him in his true colours to the men that he had consistently sold out. Little wonder then that the men followed the men who were sharing the same wage levels, the same hard work and the same working conditions as they were experiencing.

What would prove to be the final nail in Deakins coffin was the wage deal that the unions struck in 1951.

Dockworkers had waited patiently for the introduction of the Docker's charter that had been agreed and accepted by the union in 1947. It was in Liverpool that the men decided that the time had come for the union to deliver the dockers charter. After all they had shown patience beyond belief in waiting for a decent wage settlement so when the national joint council for the port industry recommended that the wages be increased by 2 shillings a day and the piece work rates be increased by up to 10% everyone expected the unions to reject the employers paltry offer.

What happened next sparked off a huge row as the union called a dock delegates conference on February the 1st and recommended that the 2 shillings a day offer be accepted. Once again the major ports found themselves being voted down by small ports that employed perhaps a few dozen mem yet they had equal voting powers as the delegates from London or Liverpool who represented many thousands of men.

When the delegates arrived back in their ports and informed the men of what had happened all hell broke out in Birkenhead and the men turned once again to the unofficial committee to lead the struggle against the deal being accepted. Joe Harrison better known to his men as "Nudger," Bob Crosby and Bill Johnson were selectively arrested under a little used law that had been brought in during the war to stop men inciting others to go on strike. The men had struck and before too long the strike had spread from Merseyside to Manchester with a few hundred London dockers showing support by joining the dispute.

It was at a meeting of the London port workers

committee being held in an East London pub that the police along with members of the special branch burst into the committee meeting to arrest a further 4 dockworkers under the same act. They were Harry Constable, Albert Timothy, Ted Dickens and Joe Cowley. The 1305 Act had been intended to be repealed by the Labour Government after the war, its main purpose was to help protect freedom and of course freedom of speech which would have disappeared had Hitler triumphed. Yet here we had a Labour Government using a war time act to stop workers exercising their right to protest and going on strike.

What the Government's actions did was to bring out another 6,700 men in London. But as the legal wrangling wore on the severity of the charges and the intent of all parties that were prosecuting became obviously ever clearer. The arrested dockworkers had been charged on three counts of incitement and conspiracy. Even more amazingly was the fact that the case was to be heard at the Old Bailey Court and as if that wasn't bad enough it was to be heard in the famous number one court. The scene of some of this country's most famous trials which usually ended up with the judge donning the famous piece of black silk before sentencing the prisoner to death by hanging!

Every time the men had to appear at court before the main trial work in the docks came to a standstill with the slogan being "When they are in the dock we are out of the dock". The men who had been arrested knew they were in deep trouble and they had to have a top barrister to present they case because the Attorney General would be leading the prosecution. The 3 Liverpool dockers selected a woman K.C (today it would be Q.C) by the name of Rose Heilbron while the 4 London dockers selected Roy Wilson as their K.C. But it would be Rose Heilbron who would steal the show with an outstanding performance.

On the first day of the trial some 8,000 London Dockers staged a strike in support of their colleagues whilst many Liverpool Dockers had travelled to London to show solidarity to their fellow dockworkers. The prosecution was led by the Attorney General Sir Hartley Shawcross who stated that these men had in defiance of their union organised a strike in Liverpool against a decision that had been democratically accepted. Further to that the defendants then travelled down to London to seek support in the form of getting them to strike against the agreement that their unions had agreed.

The men in London refused to support the Liverpool men leaving only a few hundred men in London who withdrew their labour in support of their colleagues in Liverpool. He stated that the prosecution would be calling both representatives of the Transport & General Workers Union and members of the National Dock Labour Board to give evidence against the men.

Sir Hartley Shawcross closed his opening address by stating that rightly or wrongly these men had openly and knowingly defied the law of the land in inciting the men to strike. He added that they had attempted to blackmail the country by withholding vital food supplies needed by the nation and therefor forcing the Government and the unions into scrapping an agreement that had been democratically accepted.

    Roy Wilson the London dockworkers K.C gave his response to the prosecutions opening remarks by stating that his clients had literally tried everything within the constitution of the union to get a deal in line with what was the official trade union policy namely the dockers charter that had been accepted by the union back in 1947 but had been blocked by delays and committees within the union who were listening to paid officials rather than the men they represented.

    The trial went on for days with the prosecution wheeling in witness after witness even down to the police who happened to be on duty when the mass meetings had been held that led to the walkout. The T & G.W.U gave evidence against their own men and tried to use the hearing in justifying why they had been attempting to get these men and others removed from the union. The union failed to mention why they had not pursued with as much energy in trying to get the dockworkers the Docker's charter which would have averted any need for industrial action.

    Then it came down to the closing speeches and this was where Rose Heilbron tipped by balance of the scales of justice. She asked members of the jury if the defendants should really be here. As the court was the central criminal court she asked if in fact how could the seven men be described as criminals when in fact all they were just good, honest, hardworking, decent men who were trying to get their men a deal that the official trade union should have pursued with a little more vigour. She concluded that the right to free speech had been fought for and yet the very men who had helped fight for this right now found themselves being hauled up before the central criminal court to defend themselves for the right to demonstrate the very same freedom of speech. In all her winding up speech lasted just over three hours and received widespread coverage in many of the national newspapers.

The judge for this trial was Lord Chief Justice Goddard; a judge known for handing down severe sentence's and never flinched in donning the black silk before sentencing people to death by hanging. But Rose Heilbron had done her job and the jury after coming back seeking clarification on certain points failed to deliver a verdict and it was now up the Sir Hartley Shawcross as to whether to hold a retrial. The men were released and jubilant crowds outside the court carried their leaders away from the Old Bailey singing and chanting. The Government announced that no retrial would be held and that it was their intention to scrap the 1305 Act.

Yet again Deakin had disgraced not only himself but he had used the union to pursue and hound these men and had once again failed to use the office that he held to promote and pursue better working terms for the members who paid his wages. What he had also done was to have alienated the men against the union which would once again have very serious repercussions in the not too distant future. He had used everything that was available to him in addition the Government had tried to assist him by taking the men to court. Deakin decided that he had to move himself if anything was to be done to remove the threat of communism from the industry and from the union.

So having endured several strikes that had been organised by the unofficial committees Deakin decided that whilst others may have failed to deal with the communist problem he had to set an example. He got the executive committee to expel from the union 3 men, Bert Saunders, Harry Constable and Ted Dickens. Once again the men walked out in support of their unofficial leaders after all the expelled men had only been representing the wishes of the rank and file dockworkers. What he also did to "buy off" other militant leaders he had them made up to become paid officials in the union. It's amazing how a man can change overnight once his lifestyle has improved. From being a fighter for better rights for the men he is now telling the same people he once fought for to go back to work.

Whilst on the other hand the employers did their bit to quieten anyone who may fit the militant bill by offering them a job as foreman. Again almost overnight these men instead of fighting for better rights and any increase of pay that a particular job may bring they appear to be reborn Christians as they now fend off any attempts that the men might make in demanding more pay. The old saying set a thief to catch a thief!

The 3 men who had been expelled from the union implored the men not to remain on strike but they asked that everyone join with them in getting them reinstated through the official union channels. The dock labour board also jumped on the band wagon by refusing to send the three expelled men to work or even allow them to bomp on (this was the term used for anyone who proved attendance after failing to get a job.

What Deakin and the unions failed to understand (or they didn't want to) was why the unofficial committee had such a loyal following from the men. They along with the men worked in all weathers, sometimes freezing cold and getting soaking wet because they could not afford the correct work clothes. They with the men had to work at a breakneck pace in dangerous conditions just to get a decent return for their labour. They along with the men lived in pitiful conditions often sharing a couple of rooms which led to severe overcrowding; it was not unusual for 15 or 20 people to share a small house. All these conditions contributed to the men's anger towards the trade union officials who enjoyed a more comfortable lifestyle.

But probably the underlying reason that the men were so discontented was the fact that the union had adopted the so called dockers charter back in 1947 and were no nearer getting it for the men who in paying their trade union subscriptions were paying and employing these men who were consistently selling them short and when the men decided to do something about it the very same men would come down to the docks and urge the men to work normally.

Matters came to an head when the men all reported for work with the dock labour board who had consistently refused to allocate the men to any jobs whatsoever. The men now took matters into their own hands and refused all allocations stating that until the men, who had been technically sacked, where given a job then they would not accept any work at all.

  The T & G under Deakins leadership had once again caused unnecessary trouble once again if they were allowed to get away with this who would be next? Almost overnight a solution was reached Dickens and Constable joined the Blue union while Sanders was reinstated in the T&G. When the news broke the men wanted their revenge on the dock labour officials who had consistently refused the three men's books. They once again refused all allocations until Harry Constable was given the pick of the jobs that were available that morning. A hurried meeting between the trade union officials and the dock labour officials quickly conceded to the men's demands and when Harry Constable was offered the pick of the jobs he asked what was the worst job and he then duly accepted that job! A lesson today for everyone who claim to represent the men.

  "Peace" had descended on the docks, but the so called peace was not to last too long. The unions especially the T & G had not learnt any lessons from events that had plagued the dock industry for over fifty years. Instead of regularly holding meetings with the men and keeping them informed on any events that were of interest and in doing that they could have regained power from the unofficial committees. But before they could do that they had to have something concrete to report back to the men and as they had continued their crusade in getting the communists out of the union so instead of pursuing getting the wages and conditions put right they once again fell into Deakins trap.

Further failure's to put the dockworkers wages right and the continuing hostility towards the union especially the T & G who had given evidence against the men's unofficial leaders at the Old Bailey an unforgivable action that the men would never forgive them for. Added to this and what would further drive the men into the arms of the unofficial committees was the decision taken by the T & G at its bi-annual conference to ban any communist from holding any office inside the Transport Union. This decision would stand for 28 years before it was rescinded and had been brought about by the rantings of Deakin who believed that the communists were about to overthrow a democratically elected Government.

Had the unions- especially the T & G attempted to get the dockworker's better working conditions there would have been no need for any unofficial committees but given the fact that the present day working conditions had hardly changed since the Victorian times. No place to have a wash or tidy up before going home, the few toilets were not fit for animals yet alone human beings they were not maintained and you had to be brave or desperate before using them and given the mess and the stench it was a wonder that the bubonic plague never broke out.

No overalls were supplied so if you were working on a dirty cargo like cement, flour or any of the toxic fine dust cargoes you just went home smothered in whatever dust that you might have been working. This also applied to asbestos that was shipped in paper bags or hessian sacks and as many thousands of dockworkers and their families have discovered it wasn't just the mess with this cargo because it left its legacy in the form of asbestosis a terrifying illness. You breathed it in all day as you worked it yet your family stood as much chance of contacting the illness as you only needed one small particle of asbestos that once inhaled it would lodge onto your lung and there it could lay dormant for ten or twenty years. When it becomes active you are done for a network resembling a tree grows in your lungs and slowly you are destined for a pretty nasty end.

    Not much was known about the perils of asbestos at the time and yet when the men did discover what this evil cargo was capable of inflicting on you the unions joined with the employers in condemning the men who had said that they wouldn't work it anymore accusing them of driving trade away from the port!

    Once again a local trade union official made a ruling that would cause yet more mayhem in the docks in the port of Hull. A job that had been accepted and worked as a custom and practise for decades was called into question, the men were unloading a grain ship and part of the operation would involve "hand scuttling" this was considered to be both highly dangerous and a back breaking way of discharging grain. This method of assisting the discharge of grain went back to the days of sailing ships, and when the men who had been allocated to this job questioned the way that they had to scoop up the grain and put it in the centre of the hold the union were brought in. In the port of Hull there was only one union the T & G, the blue union were based in London only.

The area union official Parnell who had been called in to inspect the method of hand scuttling quickly dismissed the men's claim to end this method of discharging grain stating that this method of discharging grain had been accepted by dockworkers for as long as he could remember and therefor he dismissed the men's claims of calling for change. The men refused to work the grain by using this method and were put of pay which in turn led to a walk out in sympathy by the rest of the men in the port of Hull.

	The union responded by not getting the employers to review this arduous and dangerous method of discharge but instead the local official Parnell condemned the men's actions and told them to return to work! That's diplomacy for you. Coupled with this at the same time was a dispute that had been festering in London for some time. It was about men being made to work overtime; if the employer wanted to finish up an operation or the ship could sail earlier than was originally planned the foreman would approach the men and tell them that they would be working a short night. This meant that a man would have to work up until 11pm and this after he had started work at 8am that morning.

	Overtime was viewed as compulsory and refusal could lead to the company blacklisting the men who had turned it down or even a suspension by the local dock labour board this would mean that apart from being blacklisted by that shipping company the men would also get three or four days suspension. The blue union were in the vanguard in trying to get this changed so that the men could either accept or turn down the overtime without any recriminations from the employers.

With the Hull men out on unofficial strike the unofficial committee from Birkenhead visited Hull to find out what was going on. The unofficial committee in Hull had made a call at the mass meeting that the men should consider leaving the T & G and join the blue union. This was met with overwhelming support from the men and when the delegation from Birkenhead heard this they convened a mass meeting and put the same proposal to the men and once again it was met with acclaim.

The blue union could hardly believe their luck and dispatched their general secretary Bill Newman with other members of the union's executive committee to Hull and Liverpool. A recruiting office was set up and over the next five months some 16,000 members had deserted the T & G and joined the blue union. Men from Hull, Birkenhead, Liverpool and Manchester had now made the blue union a national union instead of just being based in London. But if they thought that the T & G would take this lying down then they were mistaken. The T & G made sure that life would be uncomfortable to say the least for the blue union who outside London had no negotiating rights and when they applied to gain these rights in their new ports they met a barrage of resistance both from the T & G and the employers. A deal had been hatched between the T & G and the employers.

This left the blue union and its members no alternative other than to strike for recognition and on the 28th May walkouts began in London and the ports where they had established a base and gained new members. Then in a bizarre twist the executive of the blue union held mass meetings in all the ports that were affected and recommended that the strike be called off. The men overwhelmingly rejected this but the cracks began to appear as a result of the blue unions strange attitude towards what was happening. The northern ports were fairly solid with almost all the T & G members coming out in support but in London only 10,000 out of a labour force of 36,000 withdrew their labour in support of the blue union.

 The pressure that was put on to the blue union was immense and when the T.U.C instructed the blue union to end the stoppage and return all the members in the northern ports back to the T & G. The local dock labour boards not only refused to allow the blue union have a representative on the board but in Liverpool they even went as far as to dismiss from the industry three members of the blue union as they had taken up roles as paid officials in the blue union!

 During all this mayhem the blue union now called a strike and made it official on the question of compulsory overtime. This really enhanced the blue unions standing with the men. This was a victory for the blue union as the T & G had opposed any actions and had urged the men not to support the stoppage. The compulsory overtime clause was withdrawn and it was this that led many men to desert the T & G for the blue union.

 However many London men harboured thoughts that the blue union executive was in the main controlled by stevedore's who held very conservative views and as if this was not bad enough the general view that stevedore's held was that they were vastly superior to dockers. They viewed dockers as labourers. It was because of these beliefs that the stevedore's held that stopped many more men in London joining the blue union.

With the pressure mounting on the blue union and the strike was entering its sixth week the blue union executive took the unusual step of meeting with the liaison committee (formally the unofficial port workers committee) to discuss events and find a way back to work without losing face. The strike was crumbling with in the main only the hard core supporters keeping it going but the blue union had never experienced pressure of this nature and it was generally agreed that they would fight through the courts and any constitutional means that were available to them to fight for their right to be recognised. Also they would use the same machinery to protect their members who had been the subject of victimisation.

The blue union had opened union offices in many of the Northern Ports where there had been a mass exodus from the T & G. However the T &G were not done for and their first move was to stop the blue union from sitting on any of the local dock labour boards a move that would stop any blue union members from being able to get their sons a job in the docks whenever recruitment was called for. Also they found themselves on the outside of all the main negotiating committees. It would take years before the blue union won any of these rights back in their courtroom battles.

Then came another hammer blow under pressure from the T & G in March 1955 the T.U.C expelled the blue union from the T.U.C. This was because as they had not had members in the Northern Ports any recruitment was viewed as poaching members therefor under the Bridlington agreement the blue union were thrown out of the T.U.C. David and Goliath doesn't come into it.

Unfortunately for all the dockworkers that had joined the blue union looking for more shop floor leadership it never transpired. The blue union had enjoyed a relationship in London that many of the men readily identified themselves with. The blue union given its size was more able to quickly respond to what its members wanted, however when they found themselves having to take on board major decisions that they knew the T & G would oppose thus isolating them and their members they seemed to crumble.

The local boards filled their boots by dismissing blue union members in the Northern Ports with the blue union unable to defend their member's rights. Things were getting worse and a gradual drift by dockworkers back to the T & G signalled the end for the blue union. Their members had to resort to fighting for their rights in the courts without union backing. In all probability the blue union's funds could not cope with enormous court costs.

Many men who were activists inside the trade unions belonged to a wide range of political parties, this may have been because of the war and many men and women believed that by belonging to the communist party or a trotskyist or even a Marxist party it would help bring about future peace and get workers a fairer deal at their workplace. The Government and the media never saw it that way and Arthur Deakin most certainly regularly checked that there were no reds under his bed every night!

Because of widespread industrial unrest the Government relied heavily on M.I 5 to keep tabs on any union activist whether he was a bona fide trade union delegate or a unofficial member representing the men where they worked. This led to several Liverpool dockers being dismissed whilst in London the purge intensified again being orchestrated by Deakin. There were howls of protest from T & G members when they sent upwards of thirty full time officials to the northern ports in an attempt to get the members back.

Despite issuing a series of leaflets and holding mass meetings their trip was mainly in vain as hardly any returned. The T & G members who had remained in the union protested about the amount of money being spent in fighting court cases that the blue union members had been forced into. It appears that Deakin had set aside a war chest that contained unlimited funds in order to smash the blue union. His members unaware of this but knew that funds were being used asked the question of why could the union put as much effort into fighting the employers as they had in fighting another union.

This period must rank as one of the T & Gs darkest moments in its long history. Deakin absolutely ruined people's lives people who worked hard for their living, people who stepped up to the mantle and accepted the role of trying to better their workmates livelihoods. These people received neither pay nor adulations yet Deakin made sure that their lives were turned upside down in his never ending pursuit of anyone who dared stand up against both the employers and the unions. Vic Marney speaking at a mass meeting described Arthur Deakin as "a worst enemy to us trade unionists than Hitler ever tried to be "and his views on Deakin were greeted by rapturous applause.

But life is a funny old thing and it certainly throws up its fair share of strange twists. It was rather ironic that Deakin who was due to retire in November 1955 but on May Day of that year he was addressing a mayday rally when he collapsed and died before he reached the hospital. He must be spinning in his grave at the thought of dying on May Day! He was succeeded by Jock Tiffin who only lasted six months before he too died. Enter Frank Cousins.

The not so Swinging Sixties

Relative peace had broken out following the madness that had occurred in the 1950s this could be that the Deakin era had gone and that there was plenty of work. However, not much had changed when it came down to working conditions and the rates of pay. Yes there had been the local disputes but these appear to have been nipped in the bud early rather than let them get out of control and lead to a much more widespread dispute as had been the case in the 1950s. But all was not well despite the docks being full of ships which led to the dockworkers enjoying almost full employment.

No matter how you dress it up the working conditions in the docks in the 1960s where still wretched. The call on was still prevalent and the bosses still had the right to make you attend the call at 7.45 in the morning and again at 12.45pm and if you still were not able to find a job on the call then you had to report to the box (local dock labour office) to get a bomper. For this you received the mighty sum of eleven pounds a week. The call on still resembled a cattle market with men jostling to try and get the best jobs.

When you went to work the working conditions resembled something out of a Charles Dickens book, no protective clothing, no clothing to keep out the cold when you were working meat from deep freezers in the ships holds. Nowhere to have a cup of tea or a bite to eat and given the vast area that the docks were spread over you could find yourself a mile or so from the nearest café where you would have your lunch, more often than not the men resorted to a sandwich and a cup of tea for lunch and eaten either down the ships hold or in the shed where you were working.

Given that you normally worked ten hours and it was flat out for the ten hours as everything was geared around the piecework rates which meant if you never reached a certain target then your pay suffered badly. The employers used the piecework rates to their advantage to the full. Rather than give the men an increase in the basic rate of pay they sometimes would juggle the piecework rates. What all this meant was when the men took their two weeks annual holiday he only received eleven pounds a week, and by the time the rent was paid there was very little money if any to live on.

The employers used the very low basic wage to their advantage by flooding the docks with excess labour. They managed to do this because if there was a period of unemployment the wages being so low it wouldn't cost them as much as if the basic wage was in line with other industries. In some ports as many as two or three thousand men over and above what was a realistic labour strength for what that port really needed. This led to men fighting for jobs when it was quiet and in London's Royal Docks it was a common occurrence to see four or five thousand men attending the call only to discover that there were only a couple of hundred jobs.

As many of these men might have been without work for two or three weeks they were desperate to get one of these jobs and to see the call on when this happened made you wonder how low a human being has to stoop to get a day's work. Even journalists who earnt their living by consistently kicking the dockworker to death attacking the closed shop, greedy dockworkers, lazy or holding the country to ransom found it difficult to explain or justify to their readers that in this day and age men had to fight like animals to get a day's work. The irony of this is the trade unions and the employers both had to agree to recruiting levels.

Enquiry after enquiry was held into the working conditions in the docks and everyone agreed that Bevin's demand in 1930 to end the causal system that had blighted industrial relations for over fifty years. But just as every enquiry that had been held before absolutely nothing was done to rectify the wretched casual system. This was as numerous times before down to the dock employers and the shipping companies who whilst sympathising with the dockworkers in public made sure that no changes to the system that they had enjoyed for the best part of a hundred years.

Since 1955 the Government had placed their faith into a high court judge Lord Justice Devlin. He had firstly been appointed by the Conservative Government to report on whether the National Dock Labour Scheme needed any changes. He reported after meeting with all parties in the dock that the scheme should remain in its present form. This must have been a bitter pill for the conservative's and their ship-owner friends to swallow but after all the strife that had preceded the report the Tories thought that it was best left alone.

Report after report into doing away with the casual system took the industry into the mid-sixties and it was the pressure from the unofficial committees that forced the Government and the trade unions into action into actually doing something. But this time the trade union really surpassed themselves in showing how they treated their members with arrogance that belonged back in the Victorian times.

Once again after a series of unofficial strikes to try and get the wage rise that had almost been a thing of the past as far as dockworkers were concerned, it was now 1965 and the basic guaranteed wage was just over eleven pounds a week! The Beatles may have been swinging but dockworkers were most certainly not! The general secretary of the T & G had secured an even better little number for himself when Harold Wilson gave him a cabinet job, to cement this job he had to become an M.P and he secured the seat of Nuneaton at a bye election in January 1965. He then temporarily vacated the union job and Harry Nicholas took over as acting General Secretary.

Nicholas should have known more about the hardship and terrible working conditions that dockworkers faced as his own Father was a docker in Bristol. But he like Frank Cousins had slotted very nicely into the system and given the precarious working majority the Harold Wilson had the T & G leaders like many other trade union leaders tried in vain to suppress any actions that might damage

Labours chances of winning the next elections. In fact what it did was to cause more trouble as trade union members were getting fed up in hearing the unions telling their members "don't rock the boat and do anything that may damage Labour". That's fine but fancies slogans won't pay the bills and the rent.

So the Government appointed Lord Devlin to look into the pay structure and the causal scheme in the docks in 1965.This would turn out to be the blue print for the future of the dock industry. What Devlin proposed was a wage rise of nineteen shillings and two pence a week. This was if you don't mind meant to be a sweetener for what was to follow. In his report he recommended that the blue union be re-instated on all negotiating committees in order to try and wrest power away from the unofficial committees.

He also recommended that negotiations commence immediately to bring about an end to the casual system that had blighted industrial relations in the industry. Whether or not the T & G in submitting its evidence stated that non scheme ports should be brought into the scheme is not known. What is known that ports such as Dover and Felixstowe enjoyed an advantage over all the other major ports that belonged to the National Dock Labour Scheme as the employers had to pay a levy that went towards operating the scheme. The non-scheme ports enjoyed the luxury of being able to poach shipping from ports as they never had the overheads that the ports in the scheme were faced with.

This omission was to play a major role in the decline

of the dock industry as the years passed by. But the offer to increase the wages up to twelve pounds a week was an insult. How long could Lord Devlin and his muckers survive on twelve pounds a week? When the insulting offer got out the Liaison committee stepped up the pressure to obtain a decent wage and conditions that many other industries took for granted. In London the Royal Docks and the West India docks banned any weekend work with the threat of lightning strikes.

  This whole fiasco dragged on into the following year when the employers and the unions agreed to raise the basic wage to fifteen pounds in London, but it was less outside of London. But what happened next was disgraceful. It was another shameful episode in the way the trade unions treated the dockworkers. The employers and the trade unions both entered into a pact whereby they agreed to secret negotiations in their quest to introducing decasualisation into the docks.

  When the whole thing blew up in their faces later the union delegates who had been part of the secret pact said that they agreed to it as the talks were long and protracted, and all parties thought it best that rather than certain parts being released they thought it better that the whole package should be presented. What they really meant was they did not want the unofficial committees to get their teeth into what they had conceded.

  If you don't mind the trade unions heralded the secret agreement as a milestone in the history of the dock industry. What they never mentioned while feathering their own caps was what they had conceded in getting what was rightfully ours and was about forty years late in coming. Also, the document that they had already signed and agreed with the employers, without the men even being aware that talks had been taking place! Not to mention the fact that they might ask the members if the deal was acceptable to them contained two words that alarmed anyone who had any idea of negotiating. The two words that gave rise for concern were the title of the agreement it read- Phase One. Harmless enough you may think but where there is a Phase one there must be a Phase two.

But in the meantime we had to come to terms what had been agreed on our behalf without us having any knowledge of it. First of all and the most important part of the agreement was that every dockworker would be allocated to a permanent employer. This would be your regular place of work and in essence that spelt the end of the causal system. The call would no longer be of any use so that too was to be destined to the history books. A pension scheme was to be introduced with the men contributing half a crown (twelve and a half pence in today's language) a week. For this any dockworker retiring after perhaps serving the industry for thirty or forty years would be rewarded with a lump sum of a hundred pounds and a weekly pension of ten shillings a week (again fifty pence in today's terms).

The appalling terms that dockworkers were faced with included the final humiliation of no pension and no death benefit. Even if you died before you retired or were killed in an industrial accident your family received nothing. For many old dockworkers the end meant a paupers funeral or to put it in dockology terms "the nine o'clock trot" which meant that the widow who had no money to bury her husband and as such the local council gave you a pauper's funeral. This was what you got after giving a lifetime of service to the dock employers.

A group of men in the docks had seen that this was causing a great deal of distress to the families of bereaved dockworkers so they took on the herculean task of forming the distress fund. This would give the next of kin seventy five pounds when a dockworker died. To accumulate the funds required to pay out these benefits agents had to collect a shilling (5pence) a week from everyone who joined.

The shilling would be halved with sixpence going into the fund and the other sixpence giving you a chance to win in the football sweepstake. To carry out this huge undertaking agents from all over the docks were enlisted and they would encourage people to join and after they had collected the funds they then paid them in every Friday night, Every one of these men did the job on a voluntary basis. As for the men who formed the distress fund and got it up and running they deserve to be remembered for the work they undertook but most importantly for giving some dignity to the person in the form of a decent funeral.

The men who helped form the distress fund in the Royal Docks never looked for rewards or praise but when you see the honours list come out twice a year packed out with people who have done absolutely nothing to help their fellow men. The original management committee should have been bestowed the highest honour that could be awarded to them. I salute them and thank them for everything that they did week in week out. Blow is a list of names who were giants amongst their fellow workers. On behalf of every dockworker I say thank you for what you did.

Ollie Williams, Billy Knight, Harry Hickey, Jimmy McCarthy, Harry Chambers, Johnnie Barham, Tommy Ross, Davy Bryan, Danny Talbot, Don Perry, Jimmy Law and Tim Driscoll. Every one of them was a true giant. If the working class had a medal that was equivalent to the V.C every one of these men would have been awarded it.

The old boys would be treated to a Christmas dinner and a few drinks every year and it showed dockworkers in their true colours. Several of the old boys refused to take their seats around the dining table because the person in the next seat had blacklegged in the 1912 strike!! Some fifty or sixty years on and it still comes back to haunt you!

Before the distress fund was formed if a dockworker died then some of his workmates would go around the docks with a collection sheet and try to raise a few bob or the man's wife so as to help towards the funeral costs. This was very magnanimous but the down side of it was if the man who had died was not very well known then the collection sheets would reflect that as opposed to a man who was well known then people gave more freely as they knew him well. The distress fund gave everyone the same. Come the day of the funeral his workmates would attend and once again if the deceased was well known then he would be given a rousing send off!

A Docker's funeral was truly and still is in a lot of

cases an experience that you would never forget! The mourners would include many of the deceased man's workmates. They would show the upmost respect to the dead man's family. Once again the turnout would generally depend on how well the man was known. If he was a quiet person who kept himself to himself his turnout would be restricted to his everyday workmates whereas if the person who had died was very well known the turnout could well be in the hundreds.

    Generally once the service was over and the workmates would retire to a local pub and as the beer flowed so did the quips if the man had been a good trade unionist and a fighter the men's rights he would be in the "he was a lazy bastard" brigade whereas if the man just kept quiet and got on with his job he fell into the "what a greedy bastard" category. You couldn't win even when you were dead!

    I had now settled into my chosen occupation and I like many other youngsters who had followed their fathers into the dock industry was beginning to wonder if I had done the right thing. The money was alright when you had a job but I seemed to be doing a couple of days a week and the rest of the week I found myself out of work despite my best efforts. The conditions that we were expected to work under were again something that was very hard to get your head around, the amenities were almost non-existent. But what helped was that you gradually become known depending on your father's reputation and my father was held in high regard so that helped immensely. But even the dimmest of characters knew that trouble was brewing with the proposed introduction of a new deal.

But as all of this was unfolding and many dockworkers were fully aware that what the union were proposing would lead to a strike so it was a time when you needed to try and put a few bob aside for a rainy day. But before the rainy day arrived Britain's ports were hit by a hurricane in the form of the seamen's strike. On May 16th 1966 as each ship docked and the crews were paid off they then went on strike, ships were taken out of the docks to river estuary's where they would lay up until the strike was finished and then sign on a new crew.

Week after week saw the strike get stronger and stronger in Britain's major ports there was a run on the pound with the Government declaring a state of emergency -. However they were unable to put troops onto the ships as it was a different kettle of fish to a dock strike. What the seamen's strike meant for thousands of dockworkers was weeks and weeks of unemployment. The fall back wage was still a little over eleven pounds a week and whereas if you had a week or two of unemployment you had a chance to earn some money when you found a job, this was not case now and the seaman's strike went right on through June into July before it was called off on July the first. But ships had been diverted to avoid being caught up in the strike and this further added to the misery of the dockworkers who found themselves unemployed well into August. Given the paltry basic wage many dockworkers found themselves deep in debt where they had borrowed money purely to live.

If you thought that you knew what hardship was then

compare this experience with your lot today. I remember being brought up in a one bedroomed basement flat with a tiny living room and a scullery (kitchen in today's language) outside toilet and no bathroom with only cold water to wash with. You had a coal fire to keep warm as central heating was unheard of. The place was riddled with dampness, when we had used the last of the coal. My father went to the coal shed and took out the axe and went out returning some minutes later with a large solid wooden front gate. He had chopped down the neighbour's wooden gate. My mother was worried about possible repercussions but my father just brushed her fears to one side by telling her that they won't say anything as they were both deaf and dumb! Not to politically correct in those days. Anyhow we had a roaring fire for a few days! And you thought you were hard done by!

As the seamen went back the full details of the Devlin report where emerging. Things certainly did not look to clever. Not only did the new scheme not make provisions for bringing all ports into the scheme which would create a level playing field but once the scheme was accepted it would mean that all of the older dockworkers over the normal retirement age would be dismissed with the hundred pound bounty and ten bob a week pension. However this was kept back from the men until October of that year.

Many of the old boys who had passed the retirement age were able to work on doing two or three days work a week. Their duties obviously they could not do the work of an able bodied dockworker carrying out piecework so the jobs they did were of a lighter nature such as repairing busted bags or sacks, mending broken crates or boxes and opening and closing the shed doors. This brought them their beer and baccy money. Had everyone been aware that the report planned on getting rid of these men then there would have been no way that it would have accepted.

Everyone was given a choice as to which company they would prefer to work for, although there could be no guarantees many of the men did manage to work for the company that they had chosen they were sent a new identification work card from the company that they would be working for when the new scheme was to start. The men were very suspicious of what might lay ahead. Jack Dash who was chairman of the Liaison committee in London was holding dock gate meetings two or three times a week and believe me the unofficial committee were not very complimentary towards both unions and more importantly the branch delegates who had agreed to keep all the talks and developments secret.

Another change that was being muted at that time was that the T & G was about to lift the ban on communist party members from holding office of any description in the union. This seemed to lift the spirits of the communists who no doubt held meetings at their headquarters in King Street to work out who would get themselves elected and on to what committees.

However as soon as many of them got elected and they saw what had been agreed in the Devlin report they quickly abandoned ship when it would seem that they had to agree with some pretty unpopular measures. But it hadn't stopped them quickly learning some very slippery tricks or as soon as they resigned citing reasons that had nothing to do with the real reason why they had walked away and what was unforgivable was that they never told the men what really was going on in secret that would eventually lead to major trouble. In truth they were as slippery as the delegates that they had been castigating over the years!

But before all that could take place we now had a date for the end of decasualisation and the union were handing out the new agreement that they had thrashed out with the employers although as you read it seemed that the employers had given the unions a good thrashing! The concessions that had been made by the unions made the mind boggle. Not only had they agreed to all these new measures but they found no time to hold daily meetings to inform the men of the changes that had been made.

The Liaison committee seized upon this and as the day of the new agreement neared so Jackie Dash cranked up the volume and before long he had the men eating out of the palm of his hand. The unions had given up nearly every restrictive practise that we had fought for over the years for a pittance of a basic wage and it was this that the unofficial committees up and down the country seized upon. As such on Monday September 18th 1967 there was a walk out in nearly all of the country's major ports. In truth although the strike was about the basic wage the real reason was the men never liked what the union had agreed to.

Piece work would remain, the hours of work would

be the same and although every registered dockworker would now receive one additional week's holiday to be taken in the winter the pay for this would again be the basic wage. Yet it was commonly accepted that bulk of the dockworker's daily pay was made up by overtime and piecework earnings yet when it came to holiday pay instead of being paid the average wage a dockworker was presented with the basic wage. So for three weeks a year the men had to take a severe wage cut whilst enjoying their holidays!

    The strike now was gaining national support and the unions tried to get everyone back to work on a promise that they would seek an increase immediately in the basic wage. Unfortunately for them and given how they had been in secret talks therefor denying any knowledge of what was going on the men would have none of it. The unions and the employers realising the gravity of the situation held a top level meeting and the basic wage was increased nationally to fifteen pounds a week with London receiving an additional two pounds in the name of a London weighting allowance.

    This got everyone back to work however Liverpool where having none of it and they remained out on strike. They sent delegations to all the major ports to try and get support, however, Liverpool were out on strike against the new agreement and for some unknown reason the unofficial committee in London tried to stop the Liverpool men from even addressing the men! It turned out that many of Liverpool's unofficial committee had Trotskyist leanings and whilst the unofficial committee in London tended to be more communist orientated. However the men in London demanded that the Liverpool men be given an opportunity to state their case and the unofficial committee had to relent and give way. However the Liverpool delegation headed by Kavanagh and Kerrigan got no joy and so Liverpool remained out on strike on their own.

But the peace in London was very short lived in a matter of a few days after the men had rejected Liverpool's call for support when a gang of men had been transferred to company who needed additional labour. A gang of twelve men were sent to help unload a ship. Now in the docks the continuity rule was the Holy Grail in the rule book. It was to prevent the employers taking on men to unload or load a ship and when their blue eyed boys became available then they would pay of the casual men and replace them with their regular men. The continuity rule stated that once you commenced the job you stayed there until the job was completed.

When the men who had been loaned to unload a ship were paid off and replaced by the companies own men all hell broke out. The liaison committee called a mass meeting of all the men in the Royal Docks and after hearing from liaison committee members Jackie Dash and Ernie Rice the men voted to go on strike until the continuity rule was reinstated. However the rest of London's dockworkers never saw it in the same vein and barring men from the West India docks they refused to enter the struggle.

The trade unions called a mass meeting at the Royal

Docks with Peter Shea the London area docks secretary was shouted down and the van that had the loudspeakers on it was almost turned over. Shea left the meeting shook up but told reporters that he was disgusted with certain elements of the crowd. He had been supported on the platform by the paid officer for the Royal Group of docks Bill Munday and he was having none of it as he knew the mood of the men. More important was the fact that when this dispute was over and the likes of Peter Shea and company disappear back into their comfortable offices Bill Munday would have to face the men every day.

    Jack Dash always had something to keep the strikers occupied and he loved nothing better than a march! He marched the men from the Royal Docks one day up to Tower Hill and from there he led the men to Downing Street, this was before it became a fortress and people were allowed to demonstrate freely in Downing Street, when he discovered that the Prime Minister was attending the House of Commons he then marched the demonstration to Parliament!

    But as the weeks rolled on and there was no sign of the dispute being brought to an end the strike in London's Royal Docks showed its first signs of dissent when a ship from South America carrying chilled beef was docked and they managed to get some blacklegs to work it. The unions now called another mass meeting at the Royal Docks but this time they hired what appeared to be a huge furniture van that held the speaking equipment. They said to dockworkers nearby "try and turn that over!", but they hadn't counted on one of the dockers who brought a bugle to the meeting and proceeded to play it non-stop while Peter Shea once again tried to get the men back to work. The strike had now continued well into November and with Xmas on many people's minds the whole crowd at the meeting burst into song singing I'm dreaming of a white Xmas!! Even the union officers had to smile.

But there was very little to sing or smile about and the liaison committee realising that they were not just battling the employers who were in cahoots with the trade unions on this issue added to that was the fact that Liverpool had gone back after the union done a secret deal with them. The unions knew that if they could get Liverpool back then the striking men in London would feel further isolated recommended that the strike be called off.

Dashy then had a brainwave. He had put it down to the youngsters who had helped the crowd in turning over the recommendation to go back so he dispatched delegations to every main port in the country in one final effort to get support. As you could guess the most important port would be Liverpool and you would expect the big guns to take this port but Jack was having none of it and he knew that he would send the four youngsters who were giving him grief about going back.

So it was off to Liverpool on a bitterly cold night. The "lucky" four who had been sent to Liverpool were Roy Lane, Mickey Fenn, Alan Williams also known as Willie and myself. We travelled up overnight in Willies ford Anglia armed with ten pounds to cover petrol and get ourselves something to eat! Dave Timothy was the treasurer of the liaison committee, he was the son of Albert Timothy who was a grand speaker and had served on the liaison committees in the past before being tragically killed when falling down a ships hold. Now if you can survive on two pounds fifty each, plus petrol on an overnight trip to Liverpool and returning the following evening then Timmo should be the Chancellor of the Exchequer!!

When we arrived in Liverpool we were met by Dennis Kelly who was to us like the Godfather of Liverpool docks as he walked along the quayside everyone acknowledged him. No-one but no-one failed to bid him good morning or give an approving nod the man was a giant in every way. You don't just acquire respect of this nature it is earned over years of representing the men and from that Dennis Kelly built up respect that I have hardly ever seen before or since. A truly remarkable man. He was aware why Dashy had sent us rather than come himself as there was history that went back years and dockworkers have this knack of not forgetting.

Dennis told us that as the men had only just returned from a seven week strike it was highly improbable that the men would have the stomach to walk out again. He did offer us the opportunity of addressing the men, he said he realised that we were up against it and as such he would call his men to a mass meeting at the Pier Head. Now none of us had ever spoken at a public meeting and the thought of addressing the Liverpool men especially after the London dockworkers had turned their backs on the Liverpool men when they had come down to London for support. We thanked Dennis for his hospitality (he had treated us all to a slap up fried breakfast!) and headed back home.

We knew the game was up and it was only a matter of time now before we had to swallow our pride and go back to work. But something happened that gave cause for concern just before the strike ended. In the docks there is nothing worse than a blackleg. A ship had docked in the Royal Victoria Docks and it was to unload its cargo of chilled beef from South America. The company managed to find enough men to begin unloading the cargo. These men would pay the ultimate price for their deeds.

If you are out on strike any benefits or wage increases are enjoyed by the whole labour force so blacklegs should not receive any benefits that their striking workmates may have won. In the docks a scab is never forgiven people may say that there must be desperate reasons for someone to become a blackleg and scab on his mates. This is a fallacy as everyone is in the same boat. For the men who chose to scab in the 1967 strike life dealt them a very unkind hand.

Somehow or the other all the men who were working the ship found that their new identification cards had "fallen" into the hands of the wrong people. On their identification cards was their name, address and in some cases telephone numbers. Five thousand leaflets were printed with all these details and distributed at a mass meeting. For the blacklegs the game was up they received threatening calls, wreaths had been delivered to their homes and one scab just managed to stop a load of ready mix cement being deposited at his home! The employers got the police in who then got the special branch in on the case.

For the sake of a week's wages these men had ruined their lives. They could be out having a drink or enjoying a social occasion when someone might spot them and announce it loudly that he was a blackleg and he should roll up his trousers to show everyone what a blackleg looks like! It would never go away.

I was handing out leaflets at one of the mass meetings when I was about to give one to someone in the crowd when someone said to me "don't give that ponce one he's a blackleg" and with that a right hander went whistling past my face and hit him fair and square on the jaw knocking him spark out. Henry Cooper would have been proud of the punch! Such are the burdens of being a scab. The inevitable decision was taken to return to work and it probably was one of the most humiliating defeats that the dockworkers had ever endured. Jack Dash and the liaison committee marched everyone back to attempt to show defiance but the truth was that we had suffered a terrible beating. But unbeknown to us the employers had held meetings. They had decided that they should not provoke us in anyway especially if it could lead to another stoppage.

Just after the strike finished a group of longshoremen (American Dockworkers) came over to London to meet with the delegates in London to discuss containerisation. They had produced a book showing what containerisation would bring. It showed how the men had to struggle and physically exhaust themselves to earn a living by loading and unloading cargos by the conventional methods. It then showed the same cargos being worked by palletisation and containerisation, with the men loading five or ten times as much cargo without breaking sweat or getting smothered in dust.

However as they and the book pointed out this could lead to many of their members being surplus to requirements and they had struck a deal with the employers giving their members wage rises and a protected livelihood. Their members would receive longer holidays and retire earlier on a decent pension. The agreement was called the M & M agreement which stood for modernisation and mechanisation agreement. The longshoremen told us to prepare for containerisation as it would be coming in sooner than we thought. We informed them that here in London we hardly ever saw a container and that when we loaded cargo that had been palletised our manning was the same.

The longshoremen told us to prepare for containerisation and the subsequent job losses that it could bring. But as much as we knew that they were right getting the message across to the men would be another thing. Explaining what containerisation would bring to the men was like telling them that there were men from mars invading Custom House! All they knew was that there was plenty of work and many of them did not seen containers as a threat to the conventional method of work.

Most of our men saw no further than the next pay packet so when we tried to explain to them that containerisation would wreak havoc on our industry it fell on deaf ears. Taking into account that they had just endured a long strike the last thing that they wanted to hear was any talk of trouble!   So we took it up with the union and as I had now become a union delegate after the night of the long knives in getting rid of many of the delegates who had been party to the secret talks the T & G had a recalled delegate docks conference to which I represented the Royal Docks.

When I raised the subject asking why our union hadn't followed the American longshoremen's lead in trying to protect the dockworkers future over here. Tim O'Leary the national docks secretary absolutely went ballistic at me accusing me of mixing with unions that did business with the mafia and he got even more excited when asking the conference if they wanted a union that employed tactics that were of criminal actions and associating them with mafia and hoodlums.

He calmed down and explained that this union did things differently and would continue to do so and it would always put the men's interest first!! You only get one chance to speak at these conferences and once the platform has responded to your question you do not have the right to reply. Tim O'Leary's response to the question should go down in the hall of fame as the most dishonest reply ever given and it should have been carved on his gravestone.

I make no apologies for what you may think that my opinions are harsh and callous but when you read what happened over the next ten years you might have a different opinion. We paid our union subscriptions and expected that the unions would look after our interests.

How silly we were in thinking that. Men pay their union subscriptions and they expect in return that their delegates and the paid officials have the foresight to protect their livelihoods.

We had met the American Longshoremen in a room above the Connaught public house this was probably the most packed out pub in the whole of London and if you don't mind at seven o'clock in the morning you could that it was New Year's Eve! Not a seat to be had and the air was blue with smoke. Before going into the pub to meet with our American cousins I was presented with a sheet of paper by Sammy Mott now when it comes to dockland characters our Sam was in the Premier League. Here Ross put a few bob on this list for poor old Toby who died last night. Now it was Thursday morning and I had just enough money for a cup of tea and a sausage roll for my breakfast. But you never knocked a kite (collection sheet) back in the docks for if you did your name was mud.

I duly gave Sam my last half a crown and he moved on to the next person. When I went into the Connaught who was standing up the bar large as life but Toby! I saw my father and told him and he just laughed saying that Sammy Mott will go to any lengths to go a few bob to buy him and his chums a few pints of bitter before work. Another lesson!

The first rumblings were when we attempted to get Felixstowe and Dover to become under the national dock labour scheme, this failed with us being given a whole host of assurances that included the one that hoodwinked us that the Labour Government would nationalise the docks and that would include all the non-scheme ports. But containerisation was the last thing on the minds of the dockworkers as the work now was plentiful and with the employers adopting a more lenient approach towards any awards that the men may have claimed everything in the garden looked rosy. Or did it?

The never ending saga of enquiries continued and a sneaky one was that was supposed to review the pay of dockworkers consistently referred to the Devlin report as phase one of the modernisation programme. Now when you have a phase one you know that there must be a phase two. It urged all parties to get together and speed up further modernisation talks on the future of the docks. Another little oversight that our negotiators had forgot to tell us about. I had been elected along with a whole host of new delegates to sit on the various committees that represented the men who worked in the Royal Docks.

By now the general secretary of the T & G was Jack Jones who promised to change things so as the men's voices and protests would be dealt with more quickly. He also pledged that all talks should be more open and that the membership should be kept informed at all times of any negotiations. The press were petrified of him and along with Hughie Scanlon of the A.E.U (The Boilermakers Union) the press dubbed them as "the terrible twins". These two tried their level best to bring about a socialist T.U.C but were thwarted time and time again. But Jack Jones became more approachable than that of any of his predecessor's and it was he who brought about the introduction of the shop stewards in the docks.

Although a lot of the smaller wharves and docks already had shop stewards many of the major ports only had the unofficial committees to fall back on and Jones saw that if he introduced shop stewards at everyone's place of work it would eliminate a large percentage of the troubles. The great pity is that Jack Jones was hell bent on recruiting members and it would be this that caused a giant rift between him and the dockworkers.

As our wages had not seen an increase for a while and with the unions dragging their feet on the subject it was left to the unofficial committees once more to lead the fight for an increase in the basic wage. On this occasion many of the major ports all came together and a series of lightning strikes and a couple of one day stoppages brought the employers and the unions to their senses. The basic wage being sought by the men was ten pounds a day for a ten hour day and eight pounds a day for the standard eight hour day. These strikes become more and more popular with the men as they created major disruption for the employers and the shipping companies while the men only lost a minimal amount of money.

A strange footnote to these strikes was that at first in London the unofficial committee thought that they had an informer amongst their ranks because for the first few strikes in London it caught the employers out. The members of the unofficial committee would tour the docks and inform all the men working that "todays the day" and the men would then cease working and go home.

This really played havoc with the shipping company's arrangements. If a ship was due to finish loading the tugs and the pilot would be ordered and when a lightning strike was called all these arrangements were up in the air. However after a few of these strikes the surprise element seemed to have worn off and it appeared that the employers seemed to know that a stoppage would be called on a certain day.

All the members of the liaison committee trusted each other implicitly and after a couple of times after the employers had been prepared for another stoppage doubts crept in and a full enquiry was held as to how the employers were getting prior knowledge of the stoppage. It appeared that the café that all the strike committee used was owned by a former docker and whenever a lightning strike was called he was getting saddled with lots of rolls and sandwiches which he had prepared for the lunch time rush. One of the committee tipped him of as to when the strike would be called so he wouldn't order and prepare as many lunches. This was done out of friendship as the owner of the café always let them use it to hold their meetings and he never charged a penny for the use of his back rooms where the meetings would be held.

A ships foreman who used to pop into the café for a cup of tea in the morning noticed this and told his boss and the game was up! The committee informed the café owner that they could no longer inform him so he had to take his medicine with everyone else! Upon the introduction of the shop stewards the liaison committee met with the newly elected shop stewards and handed to us the responsibility of taking over from them although it has to be said that practically every one of the liaison committee became shop stewards themselves"! The basic wage had once again not been increased since the introduction of the Devlin enquiry and as many of us had predicted having given up everything in order to gain decasualisation we had no bargaining powers.

So it was left to the shop stewards to continue the struggle to get the basic wage increased and this is where the national link up with other shop stewards from all over the country really began. Although at first it was just London and Liverpool with a sole shop steward from Preston docks by the name of Norman Wright and he was a stalwart never missing a meeting never complaining about all the travelling and giving his time off up. He was a top man!

Gradually other ports like Hull and Southampton bolstered our numbers up and we had most of the country's main ports covered. When we agreed to call the first few lightning strikes the unions began to sit up and take notice. The men again recognised us in the same vein as they had viewed the unofficial committees they knew that we did the same jobs as them and endured the same hardships and we reported back to them both at company level and at mass meetings at the dock gate (it was by the Connaught Pub and the men referred to it as the stump). Very shortly I would along with many other shop stewards faced with a dilemma as to whether it was right to serve on both the union committees and the shop stewards committees. Little did I know what the union had in store for us and it would make up my mind once and for all!

Sensing that the newly created shop stewards

movement were taking over where the unofficial committees had left of the union called an official strike to get the basic wage improved. A state of emergency was declared by the Government and another enquiry was set up to adjudicate on the matter. Lord Pearson was charged with heading the enquiry and he was told to get on with it and they took evidence over the weekend and their report and findings were presented to the Government who called in both the unions and the employers and told them that the report should be accepted without any delay.

    The claim had been for a day's pay of eight pounds for an eight hour day this appeared to have been totally ignored by our negotiators when submitting their evidence. So the union called the recalled delegates back to consider the findings of the Pearson Committee. Unbelievably these delegates accepted the findings and called off the strike. In London far from getting eight pounds a day we found ourselves being awarded twenty pounds a week or four pounds a day!

    This represented a rise of sixpence per hour! History had repeated itself as the men in 1889 had won the dockers tanner and here we were some eighty years later being awarded another tanner. The delegates called of the strike and the unions thought that was that. Once again certain parts of the report had not been reported to us with the main recommendations being that the modernisation programme should be speeded up. What this did prove to me was the advice that my father had given me some years ago he told me that the only time the unions made a strike official was when the unofficial committee were gaining popularity and taking control away from the unions. Once the strike was official the whole issue was now in the hands of the unions and it would be them and not the men who would call the strike of. His advice was spot on as the union did this a few times over the coming years.

I had now been elected onto the docks group committee which came about after a spate of resignations from some very senior delegates. I was thrown into the lion's den still as green as grass and with some of the slipperiest people that you know. The docks group committee was made up by two delegates from each area in London, Tilbury, West India Docks, Tooley Street, The wharves who worked the riverside agreement had one delegate and two from the Royal Docks. Also the nonregistered ports of Dover and Felixstowe had a rep.

The docks group committee were considering a proposal from the employers to force all the old boys who had passed the retirement age and had chosen to stay on and provision had been made for these men. Many of them had worked in the docks for forty years or more and had they retired at sixty five they would have received not a penny in the way of a pension or a lump sum. What the employers were proposing was to compulsory retire every dockworker at the age of sixty five. This would also include all the men who had chosen to work on.

For many of these old boys the right to carry on working was a god send to them. It would only be 2 or 3 days' work a week and the jobs were of a light nature. It brought them a few bob on top of their state pension and more importantly it got them out of the house and they were mixing with their workmates. The employers wanted to give them a hundred pounds lump sum and ten bob (50 pence) a week pension. When the docks group committee reported this back I made my maiden speech objecting to it stating that this represented one of the biggest insults ever known in our history and that we should not even be considering this.

The other members of this committee were seasoned and hardened delegates who had spent many a year in getting elected to this committee and most of them viewed me as a loose cannon who really represented the unofficial committee, snide remarks such as "wait until you tell Jack Dash about this" or "spread the word right across the Albert Docks". But they knew that this could not be accepted in its current form. They then astounded me when they announced that the union should hold dock gate mass meetings to inform the men of what was happening. I was speechless for a moment but when I had time to reflect I thought that my presence had forced them to change. Silly me! If only I could have known the truth.

All docks held their mass meetings and the one at the Royal Group of Docks was really well attended as the men had never experienced the union keeping the men informed and the men's curiosity led to an attendance never witnessed before. The chairman of the meeting was Morrie Foley the other delegate from our docks and he was indeed a seasoned delegate of many years standing. He addressed the men and called on Bill Munday a paid official to explain why the union was rejecting this offer and it was all fire and brimstone. Such rhetoric was unheard of from these people and then the chairman called on me to add a few words. I had never spoke at a mass meeting and when he plonked the microphone into my hand I looked at the men and all I could see was a sea of faces worst still when I tried to speak it felt like my lips were moving but no sound was coming out!

    I stumbled through it stating that the hundred pound lump sum offered by the employers represented about two pounds fifty pence for every year that the men had served in the docks and that it was an insult to these men, further to that no man should be compulsory got rid of. When I finished my throat felt like a sheet of sandpaper and I wasn't quite sure if my underpants were still clean! Morrie Foley then informed me that he had not told me that I had to speak as he didn't want me to worry. I still believe he and the other delegates got a lot of amusement from putting me in the frame. Still the men endorsed our actions and everyone went away happy.

    Jackie Dash grabbed hold of me and ushered me to one side and told me that considering how they had bolted me up I had done well he then gave me some invaluable advice he said when you speak at public meetings the golden rule is to have a good look around before you speak. Try to find people who you know are sympathetic to the subject that you are going to speak on and focus your attention on them as if you are holding a conversation with them. If they are getting embarrassed move your attention onto someone else who may be nodding in agreement with what you are saying. Sound advice indeed I used his method over the years and it works a treat.

But what followed taught me more in the great university of life and it changed my whole direction in where I would spend the rest of my days fighting for the people who elected you to represent their views. The very same committee reconvened about a week later to consider the latest employers offer to make it compulsory to retire at 65. Also to compulsory retire any of the existing dockworkers who were still at work and were older than the new proposed retirement age.

As I studied the employer's proposals the only thing that had changed was the colour of the paper on which the offer had been printed! The whole thing had been jumbled about to read differently but still our old boys were to get the order of the not so golden boot. The chairman and the paid official spoke enthusiastically about the future of the industry and added that the old boys deserved to retire at 65 after giving the best part of their lives to the industry. As the chairman went round the table to get each delegates opinion on the document I couldn't believe that this was the same group of men who had rejected the previous document. Every one of them was speaking from the same song sheet saying that this was as good as we can get.

When it finally came to my turn to make observations I knew that I was a lone voice in speaking against accepting what could only be described as reading yesterday's newspaper today and thinking that it was fresh news. I waded in speaking out against it knowing that whatever I said would make no difference to the eventual outcome as they had already made their minds up. When the chairman put it to the vote I decided that I had stated my objections and perhaps I should fall in line with the rest of them.

Then Wallop! When the chairman Morrie Foley called for those in favour I duly raised my hand whilst others who had spoken in favour of accepting it kept their hands down and voted against it. I felt inwardly sick and the chairman asked me why I had voted to accept it as the vote was close and he could have used his casting vote to throw it out. They had done me up like a kipper. I never slept a wink that night and when I went down the docks the following morning and told people what had transpired Dashy told me that I was to honest to be able to deal with people like them.

I resigned from union committees and decided that the only true course for getting what the men wanted would be through the shop stewards committee. Not only did they do me up like a kipper but what was even more disgraceful was that they accepted the deal without going back to the men.

So the deal was done and all the old boys who "enjoyed" doing a few days' work where tossed aside for a paltry sum whilst the people who had negotiated the sell-out proclaimed the deal as a ground breaking piece of negotiating! They claimed that they had laid the ground for the new pension scheme that was to be introduced into the industry. The pension scheme that they raved about should have been introduced years ago and then perhaps many old dockworkers that had pauper's funeral could have departed with a little more respect.

I resigned from the trade union committees that I

had been elected onto on the grounds that the delegates who held down most of the important posts and they all belonged to the self-preservation society which came along with a free paid up entry to the mutual admiration society. This was not what our members had elected them for but they made sure that they held positions that made them look very important and as a consequence they kidded the men that they really had the men's interest at heart! I don't think so. It was the shop stewards movement for me and several other delegates who had encountered the same problems.

The priority for the national port shop stewards committee was the question of dock work. We called on all parties (Government, employers and the unions) to implement the Bristow report that had looked into the definition of dock work and had recommended that all work within 1 mile of the river should be deemed dock work. This would have brought many container bases into the dock labour scheme and with it would have stemmed the flow of redundancies and given us a little more job security.

Many of our employers had invested their money into these containerbases purely to get out of the dock labour scheme and where using these containerbases to engage cheap labour although the shipping companies and their conservative friends denied this repeatedly, however the facts spoke for themselves and they were grossly underpaid and what was even worse was that many of them were working under terrible working conditions. Yes the shipping companies and the stevedoring contractors had found a way out of the dock labour scheme.

Just as bad was the fact that the first set of employers to embark on this campaign showed that they had the scruples of sewer rats for what they all did was once they had secured their investment in one or more of these container bases they then dispensed with their dockworkers as if nothing had happened at all. They would cite a whole raft of phoney excuses ranging from loss of trade, blaming the unions for over manning and the classic excuse was when they put up containerisation as the reason for getting rid of their labour force! No mention was ever made about how they had invested millions in the containerbases that that they were claiming as the reason that had led to their demise.

Another group had entered the affray that would accelerate the attack on the dock labour scheme and this time the employers would become the victims along with the labour that they employed. The groups were known as asset strippers and among their numbers were some very prominent people. The biggest group that engaged the use of asset stripping was Slater Walker group owned by Jim Slater and cabinet minister Peter Walker. What these toilets did was to send a surveyor unbeknown to the wharf owner to plot how much the riverside wharf was worth to them in developing the wharf into riverside apartments.

Once they had the surveyor's report they would swing into action firstly they would offer the owner of the wharf a sum of money that he would probably take a few years to earn and given that it was a lump sum the money came without all the hassle of being an employer and trying to get ships or barges to unload at your wharf. Never mind the fact that the owner may be a third or fourth generation to own the wharf, never mind the fact that through the dockworkers that they had employed had seen them earn vast profits over the years. No they couldn't wait to accept the dirty money that these asset strippers were offering.

Another member of the asset stripping club was Jimmy Goldsmith later to be rewarded for his sterling efforts in building up a fortune through other people's misery with a knighthood. He most certainly was not going to miss out on the opportunity of earning vast sums by snapping up riverside wharves and selling them on to developers. The seeds had been sown and the vultures were circling over the docks!

What made these and future employers such obnoxious people was the fact that once they dispensed with their labour force they were then returned to the national dock labour register for reallocation to another employer. Among the earliest to fold was the East India Docks a relativity small dock and was one of the first enclosed docks to be built they are now part of the huge Canary Wharf complex, then the Surrey Commercial docks folded citing a major downturn in the timber and paper trade. This vast area was quickly snapped up by developers and it later became known as Tobacco Dock a huge shopping and leisure centre.

Still the unions stalled on getting to grips with the core reason for the decline in our trade-containerisation. They told us that they were taking these employers who had opened containerbases up away from the docks to the high courts and that they had high hopes of getting a successful outcome! What they refused to listen to was that the High Courts and then the Court of Appeal and finally the House of Lords never had a track record of favouring the dockworkers over their learned friends and as for the House of Lords well when pigs can fly and West Ham win the champions cup I will believe we have a chance!

    However what all this did was to cost us valuable time whilst the wheels of "justice" ground almost to a halt sometimes. In all using the legal system cost us three very valuable years and it was the T & G led by Jack Jones who began to sound like a long playing record in stating and restating "let us use the legal system". What the T&G should have done was to call a national dock strike whilst the problem was still in its infancy. Added to this and to further complicate an already growing problem was Jack Jones relentless goal of making the T&G a giant of a union, his obsession of getting thousands of new members every month which included the workers in nearly every container base this was against our advice.

    We saw that if these workers were also members of our union we would not only be in conflict with the owners of the container bases but also our union. Also these workers only joined the union when they heard that we were claiming the work as what was rightfully ours. There was never anything sinister about our claim firstly the loading and unloading of a container is the same operation that dockworkers had carried out for decades in loading and unloading cargo into and out of the ships hold.

The loading and unloading of containers did not magically turn into non dock work overnight because the operation was being performed away from the docks. The most important part of our declaration was that we never intended nor would we allow the existing workers would not be sacked or replaced by registered dockworkers. We wanted the existing workers to be brought under the dock labour scheme.

This part of the national stewards claim was never given any media coverage in fact the newspapers along with tory politician's claimed that dockworkers were bully boys who wanted the jobs in the containerbases which would lead to the existing workers being sacked. Nothing could have been further from the truth and even when we managed to meet some of the workers in containerbases to explain this to them they refused to believe us. We told them that their working conditions and their rates of pay would dramatically improve but still they refused to believe us. But whilst all of this was going on something else was taking place that would shake the industry to its core.

The Benefits of Modernisation

The unions and the employers encouraged by the Government were negotiating phase two of the modernisation programme and Jack Jones was fully aware that all talks should be open with regular report backs to the members. This was a breath of fresh air for our industry. But the outcome of these talks led one to believe that the employers and the union delegates must have been on something for anyone who had any sense at all would never have come up with a document like they had negotiated.

What they proposed was ending the forty hour week by introducing a two tier shift system that would see you alternate weekly from an early shift to an afternoon shift. The new hours of work would be from 7 a.m. until 2 p.m. then the following week 2 p.m. until 9 p.m. This was a major breakthrough in British industrial agreements a thirty five hour week. The basic pay was to be £36.50 a week. Also it saw the total abolition of piecework. The removal of practically every restricted practise that we had.

The final decision would be taken by the men in a secret ballot. Although the delegates who had negotiated the agreement along with many of the more senior shop stewards recommended to the men to accept the document some shop stewards saw the agreement as a means to the end- why all of a sudden did the employers want to pay a decent basic wage and why did the employers guarantee you these wages whether you done one ton of cargo or a hundred tons of cargo.

    If you remove all incentives then you remove the desire to try and achieve a target. Paying the men the same daily basic wage for doing a small amount of work would indeed lead to the men doing a small amount of work as there was now no incentive to do a large amount of work. What was going on?

    A group of shop stewards issued a leaflet urging the men to reject the document pointing out the pitfalls in giving everything up and not having any incentive to work would lead to our wages being eroded over the years as we had very little left to bargain for and although they welcomed the end of the piece work system you had to have some incentive built into the new agreement. The men rejected the offer by an overwhelming majority.

    Added to the 35 hour week and a high basic wage was the bonus of receiving holiday pay at the same level that you would receive throughout the year, this ended the dreaded two weeks holidays when your pay reverted to the paltry basic wage which in every sense of the word meant that for two weeks you would accrue debt. Also the employers undertook to build amenity blocks and showers on top of the sheds. This was a first and they would supply snacks for the lunch breaks!

Further to all this they also introduced one of the finest pension schemes boasting that it was a forerunner in pension schemes and ranked amongst the best in any industry. The print workers' pension scheme was probably the best but as we all know Bob Maxwell milked it until he decided that having cleaned the scheme out it was time to take a cruise on his yacht and commit suicide leaving thousands of print workers without any pension at all. I suppose taking that on board we have to be thankful that the shipping companies never raided our pension scheme.

However given all these benefits that the employers had seen fit to give to us you had to ask yourself the obvious question and that was what is going on? The employers were forever telling us that our output was to low and yet here they were giving us a high basic wage and removing all semblance of piece work. You could understand the removal of piece work but not to have any bonus scheme whatsoever was suicidal.

Once again a group of shop stewards in London saw through what was going on and they issued a leaflet calling on the men to reject the whole deal. The trade unions were so confident of the men accepting the deal that they treated any hostility towards the scheme as irrelevant and never bothered to issue their own leaflets. The committee that had negotiated the deal had in the main come from the ranks of the shop stewards and had been reporting back and holding meetings to report any progress that they had made.

The shop stewards who had been instrumental in opposing the new deal were asked by the union why they had shown such hostility to the deal. The unions pointed out that whilst accepting that the deal was long overdue it would bring about the end of all the bad working practises that had bedevilled our industry for over hundred years or more. When asked why they had gone along with the employers in removing any form of incentives for the men they went on the attack stating that piece work had caused more accidents and deaths over the years and asked if we wanted to be party to such working practises.

We responded by agreeing with them on that front but asked why a bonus scheme could not have been put into the new deal, The stewards who opposed the deal added that without any incentives output would plummet and that in turn would further add to our woes in the form of shipping companies speeding up containerisation which would hasten the end of our industry. The trade unions thought that we were living in cuckoo land.

The shop stewards who opposed the deal also foresaw the end of an industry where the men all stuck together and if a struggle was called for in taking on the employers then you had to look far and wide to find a group of men who could match the solidarity of the dockworker's and by introducing a two shift system the labour forces would be split into two groups with men who had worked together for years becoming strangers overnight. We could see the reason that the employers wanted to distance and further dilute a labour force that had stood up to them since 1889 and had stood together in the face of both defeat and victories.

     Whilst all this was going on the shop stewards had been meeting more regularly in Birmingham on Saturdays and these meetings were becoming more regular as they saw that the threat of containerisation was speeding up at an alarming rate. It was about this time when the law lords delivered what was their most atrocious decision. The Court of Appeal had heard the unions claim for extending the dock labour scheme to include container bases within a mile of the docks this was in line with the recommendations of the Bristow report, a court of enquiry set up by the Government to try and sort out the problem of containerbases. The appeal court had heard a test case against a company in Cardiff. The company in question was the Parker packing company and they were typical of the hundreds of companies springing up all over the country doing our work.

     The Transport & General Workers Union who had repeatedly told us that they would get our jobs back by using the legal system where about to receive a hammer blow as the law lords delivered their verdicts. You can only assume that the appeal court judges must have drunk the local tavern dry whilst they considered their verdict. The appeal court judge ruled that once the cargo has left the hook of the crane then that is where dock work ends. Now further than reclaiming our work that was being lost this besotted wretch of a judge ruled that in theory the employers could employ non registered labour to do our work on the quayside!! What this ponce knew about dock could easily be fitted on the back of a postage stamp with plenty of room to spare!

The National Port Shop Stewards went berserk at the unions who claimed that they had instructed their legal teams to appeal the decision to the House of Lords. If you never actually witnessed this and someone tried to tell you that this was taking place you would not believe them. We had lost over two vital years whilst all this was trundling through the courts and still the unions where avoiding the inevitable the only way that we would reclaim our work was by direct action.

As for the appeal to the House of Lords well Lord Vestey and his shipping company friends were hardly likely to find in favour of the dockworkers. But the union was adamant that we had to exhaust the legal channels before we could consider our next move. More valuable time lost.

Meanwhile back on the modernisation front

the agreement to give us what we should have rightfully had some twenty or thirty years ago had been rejected in a postal ballot by the men. The unions could not believe that this was happening and quick as a flash Jack Jones got involved himself in reopening talks to see where everyone had gone wrong.

Before you knew what was happening another two pounds a week on the basic wage was pulled out of the hat and this time the unions left nothing to chance and issued leaflets explaining why the men should accept the deal and they called mass meetings to explain what the new deal meant to the men. This time the ballot overwhelmingly accepted the new agreement.

Jack Jones issued a statement to the Port Newspaper in which he declared that in accepting this deal Dockworkers would have security of employment and for the first time they would now be able to obtain a mortgage. This statement was on a par to Prime Minister Chamberlain's piece of paper declaring peace in our time! Jack Jones would rue the day he ever uttered those words, but it had done the trick with the men accepting the new deal. The undertaker was beginning to screw down the coffin lid.

So with the new scheme about to be implemented and with the Transport Union totally ignoring our pleas in not recruiting the workers in the containerbases things were not what the most optimistic of chaps would describe life as a bowl of cherries! But as a dockworker would always say onwards and upwards and just to prove a point to both the employers and the trade unions output plummeted when the new scheme was implemented. Tonnages fell to such an alarming low that as one dockworker put it "I can come to work now in my best clothes!" The employers sent for the shop stewards to try and rectify the matter but refused point blank to introduce a bonus scheme.

    Now you don't have to have a degree in industrial relations to know that if you pay a man the same wage for doing a job whether he produces a lot or a little then he most certainly isn't going to sweat buckets.

    The benefits of modernisation were gradually beginning to speed up and outside of the new agreement the future looked very bleak for the registered dockworker. Containerisation was growing at an alarming rate and unlike our American cousins we never had an agreement that would help protect our livelihood and to make matters even worse the main dock union, the T & G were recruiting the very men into the union who were doing our work. The importance of the national port shop stewards was now more evident as the unions still of the opinion that the case would succeed in the House of Lords. When someone asked Jack Jones what he was on he again never saw the funny side of the remark and told everyone that if they thought it was a joke he certainly didn't.

The shop stewards then informed him that in our opinion we had more chance of this country putting a man on the moon than our appeal being successful in the House of Lords. To show that we meant business in trying to get our jobs back we held mass meetings in all the major ports and the men voted to a man to hold a one day strike.

This was not the answer in trying to secure our jobs but when your backs are up against the wall you lash out. The strike was a total success but the shop stewards knew that striking would not be the answer and they continued to meet almost every Saturday in Birmingham to try and find a way that would force Jack Jones and the T & G into doing something.

Yet amidst all this strife the dockland humour still continued at a rate of knots. You can see where John Sullivan got much of his story lines from you only had to sit in a dockland café or pub to hear better humour than the top comedians used to get their laughs. It wasn't just confined to the cafes and pubs either if you listened to the banter while the men were working you would end up in fits of laughter.

The characters in the docks should have had a blue plaque erected in memory of services in dodging work while they told stories and jokes! You knew that while they entertained you they couldn't be doing their work. But the dock was awash with characters who could keep you entertained from the early hours until the end of the day.

My father managed to work extremely hard and keep everyone amused well nearly everyone I was the exception on one particular day. I went into 33 shed in the Royal Albert Docks where we had been employed on the quay unloading lambs from a ship that had just docked after a trip to New Zealand. I saw a large gathering of men all cheering and urging this chap on who had got into a confrontation with someone.

All was well until I saw the bloke doing the shouting and pushing just happened to be my Father and the man he was having a go at just happened to be one of the hardest men in the docks! He had absolutely no chance if a fight broke out and I knew that as my Father was in trouble I would have to steam in knowing that this bloke would not only knock my Father out but he would make mincemeat of me too.

My Father being urged on by all his mates continued to shout at the man that he was fed up doing his work and that he was a lazy bastard. The man not normally known for showing restraint kept on saying to my Father go away before I knock you spark out at this point my Father stopped the verbal onslaught and asked the lad if he was any good at fighting. The villain was slightly taken aback with this and he calmly told him that everyone knew that he could fight, my Father then delivered the coup de grace when he asked him if he could become his manager and arrange his next fight to which everyone burst out laughing and the man knew he had been mugged! When I say everyone was laughing I don't include myself.

Another of his classics was he told anyone who wanted to hear that when he died he had made arrangements to carry on working. Anyone silly enough to challenge him would then be told that he was to be cremated and his ashes would be put into an egg timer!

If you looked for sympathy in the docks then you had a very long wait although the dockworker was known for their solidarity and they would rally round to help one of their own who might be in trouble that's where it ended. One man had suffered a horrific accident causing him to have his neck broken and this had left him with his head permanently facing upwards leaving him looking up all the time. When I first saw him I asked my father what had happened rather than go into all the details he just said to me that his wife had run off with an airline pilot and he was looking for him!

There were no politically correct people around then to point out the terrible social conditions that existed then. Housing was at a premium and slums were rented out with landlords demanding key money and extortionate rents for a couple of rooms that would put the landlord in jail today if they tried to rent them out. Wages were terrible and working conditions were even harsher but no one stood up for the dockworkers then they wondered why dockworkers shied away from the newspapers and media people. All they wanted to do was to portray the dockworker as a lazy overpaid worker who was always coming out on strike.

But we had moved on from these terrible times and with the introduction of the second phase of the modernisation programme which had seen the dockworkers get the conditions that many other industrial workers had enjoyed for years. It would be however very short lived as the employers had drawn up plans that showed the dockworkers had not been included in any future ventures that the stevedoring contractors and the shipping companies. Of course these plans were highly secret and the employers continued to deny any wrongdoings and even assisted in sitting on committees with the unions showing that the Port of London had a future albeit with many changes to working practises.

While they participated on these committees the employers were investing heavily into containerbases how two faced could they get? History shows that the Conservative Government and the employers were working out how and when they could strip the dockworkers of their registration but as one think tank reported back to the cabinet they thought that the union might swallow it but the national port shop stewards posed a grave threat to any plans that might see the registration changed or removed. However none of this was in the public domain at the time so we had to try and get the unions on board with us in our crusade to claim back what was our work in the shape of containers being loaded and unloaded away from the docks.

The national port shop stewards committee seemed to be forever visiting Transport House the head office of the T & G to try and get Jack Jones to get the union to do something to stem the flow of jobs being lost to outside containerbases which just led to the voluntary severance gradually being increased and for anyone who was in their mid to late fifties saw this as a golden opportunity to get hold of a few bob. The unions were quick to point out that a man would never be able to save this much even he worked up to his retirement age.

With the introduction of the new and improved pension scheme that also had a death benefit payable to any dockworkers next of kin the need for the distress fund had become less urgent but they continued their sterling work in arranging Xmas dinners that brought all the old boys together. But as severance pay had reduced the amount of members with the same reason being responsible for the diminishing number of agents who tirelessly collected the men's subscriptions every week.

Whilst all this was going on there was a fund that had been set up by the trade unions that was commonly known as the tupenny fund. The fund came about in the late fifties when the employers granted the men a wage rise but unlike most other workers dockworkers never had a weekly wage; their money was made up by eleven turns. A turn was each half a day plus Saturday morning. So the wage award saw two pence left over and as you can't divide two pence elven ways. So the two pence was paid into a fund and left to accrue over the years.

When decasualisation was introduced in 1967 the fund stood at over six hundred thousand pounds. The employers topped it up to a million pounds and a committee was formed to invest it and the unions had the tricky job of asking the men how it should be spent.

So many different suggestions where put forward with ideas ranging from a holiday centre for the retired dockworkers, a grand share out and one suggestion was to bet the lot on a horse! In the end the unions came up with the idea that all the old boys who had left the docks before the severance pay had been introduced should get a share out of the interest every Xmas.

This went on the many years and as the old boys passed on the unions gradually brought into the scheme the dockworkers that had left with the smallest severance pay. This continued right up to the end when it was decided to smash it all up interest and the one million pounds and share it out to the old boys. The same fate befell the distress fund and they wound it up again with a huge party for the old boys and all the agents with the nucleus of the funds being distributed amongst the olduns.

Back on the industrial front the House of Lords better known as the house of Corruption duly delivered its verdict on what should and what not should be deemed dock work. They upheld the drunken wretch's verdict in the Court of Appeal that dockworkers had no claim to any work once the cargo left the ships hook! Jack Jones was devastated his last roll of the dice had come up snakes eyes! Would he and the executive council now listen to us? The national port shop stewards all held mass meetings and called a one day national strike and asked the men to attend Transport House where we would call on the unions to take over the reins of the battle to get back our work.

But once again our dispute was side tracked as we now had a Conservative Government led by Ted Heath whose Ministers wasted no time at all in picking up Barbara Castles failed legislation on curbing the trade unions. She had tried to tie down the trade unions with her white paper In place of strife. Her successor was Robert Carr and he wasted no time in picking up the failed bill and adding penalties to any trade union whose members maybe be taking action.

This bill gave the employers recourse to a new court where they might get an order calling on any strikers to cease any actions that could harm the employers and should the workers ignore the court order then the union that the men belonged to would be held responsible whether the actions were official or unofficial. The court then could fine the unions huge amounts of money and impose further fines for every day that the court order was ignored. The national industrial relations act as it was known further called on all unions to register with the new court. True to form the TUC and nearly all of the unions led demonstrations against the new act. Huge marches with brass bands with prominent trade union leaders making rousing speeches.

Yet behind the scenes many trade unions were moving their assets overseas and transferring any property that they owned into trust funds. Some unions even registered with the new court. The rats were deserting the sinking ship even before the SOS had been sounded! These turncoats tried to justify what they were doing by insisting that they were protecting their member's funds. Just as well the Tolpuddle Martyrs and many great working class leaders before them never adopted their views.

The national port shop stewards once again visited Transport House in a final attempt to get the union to lead the campaign to regain our work. Dear old Jack Jones was looking weary now and he asked us that rather than work as an unofficial body why we all didn't throw our weight behind the union! As many of us had held union posts before and had witnessed first-hand at the slowness and caution that the union displayed we were gob smacked at his suggestion.

We again asked him why he was recruiting

members who were working in these containerbases. His reply again was as astonishing as the previous answer he just said if our union doesn't accept them another union will sign them up.

We knew the game was up as far as the T & G was concerned it was all over. They had dragged their feet and cost us vital time by dragging the whole thing through the judicial system and having lost the case they now they turned their backs on the very section of men who had formed the union. Jack Jones and his executive committee were on a crusade to get as many members into the union as possible. They had for some reason known only to them turned their backs on probably the strongest section of the union by recruiting as many men as they could who were working in containerbases doing our jobs.

The men who were working in the containerbases were only ordinary working class people and we had no grudges with them but they had this misconception about us and our aims. Not only did they think that we wanted them to be sacked and replaced by us but the employers put their two-penneth in by stirring up the men with a pack of lies about what we intended to do if we ever got the rights to work these bases.

The truth of the matter was that we never intended for one moment in getting anyone the sack despite our assurances to this end the workers in these places chose to believe the employers rather than us. We tried to explain to them that their wages were far lower than that of a registered dockworker hence the reason that the employers had chosen this venture to be operating outside the docks.

We also told them that their working conditions would be greatly improved but again they chose not to believe us. In hindsight you could not blame them for they were convinced that we were after their jobs and I suppose anyone with that sort of threat hanging over their head would react in the same way.

So it was down to the national port shop stewards to take up the fight as the unions were frightened out of their lives of the new industrial relations court. The court had now been set up in London's Chancery Lane under a very good friend of the Conservative's a high court judge by the name of John Donaldson or as he was known to his friends Black John. The court issued guidelines that would make everyone feel at ease by stating that the normal practise of wigs and gowns should be done away with thereby making people feel more comfortable!

This court represented the most anti trade union move that any government had legislated since the beginning of time. If the workers be it official or unofficial took action against their employer then all the employer had to do was to apply to this court to seek an end to any actions. Never mind what may have caused the workforce to take any actions. Should the labour force choose to ignore the court's ruling and history shows that workers don't like high courts telling them what to do then the employers then had the right to seek damages against whatever trade union the men may have belonged to.

The trade unions now had their excuse to do nothing as they were afraid that the union's assets would be seized. Quite a few trade unions transferred their funds to overseas banks and the court also had the powers to seize any property that the union may have. So if anyone was looking for a lead from their trade union then you had a long wait. The shop stewards were now meeting almost every Saturday to come up with a solution that would be acceptable to our men.

A strike was quickly ruled out as we thought this would be playing into the hands of the newspapers and the television who would give blanket coverage that would not be sympathetic to our claims. Not that we ever expected the media to be sympathetic to our cause they would just kick us to death.

As Dashy once said beware of the media who were slapping you on the back and praising you up for tomorrow they would be stabbing you in the back and destroying you. Never a truer word was spoken. The journalists who peddle the filth that is churned out daily should be ashamed to hold a national union of journalist union card. They consistently hide behind the story that it's the editor who changes the story. We knew that the press and television were lying in wait for us.

Back on the docks the work was disappearing at an alarming rate, containerisation was now taking hold. It was a cancer and something had to be done before it got to the terminal stage. More and more men were being paid for doing no work, all the other docks had now ceased trading and had either closed down or had been mothballed(another explanation for awaiting for closure), most of the men had been absorbed into the only two main docks left the Royal Group and Tilbury. Even the dimmest person could see that it was only a matter of time before the inevitable.

The shipping companies who owned the stevedoring companies were really getting fed up with the ever increasing costs that had been imposed in the form of the NDLB levy to help finance the severance scheme. Despite them making loud noises you never heard them once make reference to the fact that the carnage that had hit the dock industry was purely of their making. It was they who had invested the profits that the dockworkers had helped them achieve in containerbases. Had they arranged for the operations to be carried out in the existing docks then there would be no cause for concern. It was also they who freely entered into a new agreement guaranteeing a high basic wage whether you did little or no work at all absolute madness.

Then out of the blue one of the largest employers in the Royal Docks announced that they were to cease trading. The company in question was Southern Stevedores who employed best part of a thousand men and it was no coincidence that Southern Stevedores just happened to be owned by Blue Funnel Line, Glen Line and Furness Withy. Just for the record these shipping companies invested fifty million pounds in forming Atlantic Container Lines (ACL). They traded mainly in the Far East.

So we now had some one thousand men dumped on the NDLB pool despite Jack Jones assurances some two years earlier that the dockworker had security of employment and as such you could now go and get a mortgage! Had you taken Jacks advice and taken out a mortgage you were in real trouble because your wages had just plummeted to a little over eleven pounds a week from what you previously earnt which was some thirty four pounds a week. Anyone who had taken Jacks advice would be facing eviction now!

A.C.L owned containerbases that ranged from Thurrock near Tilbury, Birmingham, Leeds, Aintree, Manchester and even one in Scotland. This was a clear declaration of war by these shipping companies and they appeared to be growing in confidence which was shown in the way they were now acting. Who else could sack a labour force of over a thousand men and perform the operation that the sacked men had done for decades a few miles down the road with a brand new labour? The ship-owners were flexing their muscles. What was the trade unions response? Not much they increased the severance pay to get rid of a few more unwanted dockworkers. The time had come for something to be done to arrest the situation.

The national port shop stewards met again and pooled all their ideas on how best to try and win back our work. Listening to the shop stewards from all the other ports it was obvious that the cancer called containerbases was spreading nationally at an alarming rate. We knew that if we never took action then the last rites would be performed over our industry and the people who we paid our subscriptions to in order that they look after our interests would then shrug their shoulders denying that they had done very little to protect our livelihood's.

Every shop steward was told to report back to their respective ports and get ideas on how best we should tackle the problem. It was generally agreed that we should rule out strike action as this would only punish the dock employers who were still trying to employ registered dock labour as opposed to those who had dumped their labour force onto the national dock labour pool and moved their operations outside the docks and employing non registered labour.

As a last roll of the dice in an effort to get the Transport Union onside it was suggested that we call a 24 hour stoppage and get as many men as we could to demonstrate at Transport House. See what Jack Jones and the executive committee had to say about their non-participation in trying to protect our livelihoods. The men up and down the country were now fully aware of the threat of losing their jobs and as a result they subsequently endorsed our call for a 24 hour stoppage and a large gathering of men assembled at Transport House where Jack Jones received a deputation and had questions fired at him from all directions he failed dismally to give us any reassurances that the union would take over the reins from the national port shop stewards. He appealed to us not to take any action that may lead to the union's funds being attacked by the new industrial relations court.

Never mind us losing our jobs so as long as the union's funds are O.K.!!On a lighter note when the demonstration was over at Transport House many of our men retired to the local public house.

Given that Transport House was situated in Smith Square, Westminster and the Conservatives and many well-heeled members of society had their offices nearby it came as a culture shock to many of them when they retired for their lunchtime drink to see their local full with Dockers. When the landlord came out with a huge freshly cooked gammon to put in the sandwich display cabinet it disappeared faster than an express train! Everyone had their fill and the guvnor of the pub never had a clue as to where it had gone!

So we knew that we were on our own. Any action that we might take would be without any support from the unions all we could hope for was to deliver such a punishing blow to the parties involved that they would have to do something. The shop stewards met again in Birmingham and began pooling ideas as to what action we could take. Every port was by now showing a surplus of labour this being the direct result of containerisation which had speeded up at an alarming rate. It was generally agreed that an all-out strike was out of the question but what to do? This was a real poser and as we had never been faced with this kind of problem before it took a few meetings before someone came up with an idea that most of us thought it could be a runner.

Many of us wanted to refuse to load any containers that had come from the containerbases that we were claiming as our work, however this was not the greatest idea in the world as it would put all the onus on a few docks and trying to establish just were the container had come from would prove almost impossible. So it was then that someone suggested that we picket these containerbases and ask the lorry drivers not to cross our picket line as the work inside the depot was dock work being carried out by non-registered labour. If the lorry driver then chose to break the picket line the men picketing would then make a note of the name of the haulage company and that company would be blacked in every port that the national port shop stewards were active in.

This was generally agreed as the best proposition that we could come up with and the beauty of it was it involved the men from start to finish. If they wanted to protect their jobs they now had to do their share of picketing and ensure that any haulage companies that had fallen foul of our action would not get loaded or unloaded at the countries major docks. What we all agreed was that each port would nominate two containerbases that were adjacent to their docks and that port would be responsible for picketing their two containerbases.

Every port would hold mass meetings to report this back in full and get the action endorsed by the men. The men readily agreed to all the proposals in every port. The national port shop stewards met again to finalise the details. In London we selected Hays Transport a large container base owned in part or wholly by Hays wharf who had sold all their wharves to property developers after returning their entire labour force to the unattached register.

The other one needed no explanation at all it was Midland Clod Storage Depot owned by the not so good Lord Vestey. In Liverpool one of the two that they selected was Heaton's Transport While Hull decided that the largest perpetrator in their area was a company called Panalpina who were the largest groupage depot around Hull docks. Southampton chose a couple while Preston also attacked the largest container base in their area.

The T & G never tried to stop our intended actions which given that they had members in the three targeted sections of the union the first would be the lorry drivers who belonged to the road haulage section of the union and then you had the workers in the container bases who had been recruited into the general workers section of the union and finally our own members who were founder members of the union and belonged to the docks group section of the union.

As Laurel and Hardy would have said another fine mess you've got me into! As the picketing got under way many of the lorry drivers chose to ignore our pickets and drove into the bases that the dockworkers were picketing believing that we were only bluffing.

The big players in the T.U.C had not registered with the industrial relations court but this did not stop John Donaldson and his merry men from relieving the T & G of thousands of pounds in fines. So much so that the T & G tried a clever manoeuvre by appealing the decision of the Industrial court to the court of appeal stating that shop stewards who were taking unofficial action were not carrying out the official policy of the union. Lord Denning agreed with them and overruled the industrial courts findings but the Government appealed this decision and took it to the House of Lords who overturned the appeal courts findings. Would the T & G never learn?

Go to Jail and do not collect £200

Once the haulage firms discovered that the dockworkers meant business and their entire fleet of Lorries were blacked in all the major ports they came running to meet with the stewards to find out how they could be removed from the famous "cherry blossom" list. What was happening was that once a lorry had crossed the picket line the pickets having made a note of the Lorries registration number and the name of his company would then phone the details through to the duty stewards who would place that company on the next day's cherry blossom list. The list was refreshed every day and the only way a company could be taken of off the list was to submit on the companies headed notepaper giving an undertaking that their drivers would not cross our picket lines ever again and it had to be signed by a director of the company.

In Hull Panalpina tried through the local courts to get a restraint order against Walter Cunningham the chairman of Hull port shop stewards when he failed to appear and take no notice of the courts orders they imposed a fine on him. This was a waste of time because he had no intention whatsoever in allowing a cowboy firm who was responsible for thieving his members jobs take him to court and get him fined. Everyone expected that once the fine had not been paid the next move would be to cart him off to jail.

Then Heaton's in Liverpool made their move they applied to the industrial court citing the T & G to be held responsible for the actions of their shop stewards and surprise John Donaldson agreed with them and duly fined the T & G £55,000. Get hold of that Jack Jones and added a rider saying as the union had not appeared in his court he would issue a sequestration order. So this court would seize the entire funds of Britain's largest trade union. Jack Jones asked or a better explanation would be to say he begged the T.U.C to allow the union's solicitor's to represent them in the court to which they agreed. Things were beginning to hot up.

It was at this time that the T & G through a local paid officer called the shop stewards from T. Wallis in the Royal Docks in to deliver another bombshell. The officer in question was Bill Munday and he informed the shop stewards that their employer Tom Wallis had sunk a considerable amount of money into a container base a couple of miles away. The shop stewards at that company then called for a meeting with the company's owners, Ben Line Steamers and Tom Wallis an old fashioned stevedoring contractor.

Tom Wallis got really upset when the shop stewards rattled out his investment in this company. The company in question was London East Inland Clearing Depot. It was better known as Chobham Farm. Tom Wallis became very agitated and made several outbursts about it not being anyone's business where he invests his money. The shop stewards at this company then asked the London Port Shop Stewards if Chobham Farm could be included in the container bases to be picketed. This was quickly agreed.

So the shop stewards at Tommy Wallis's made it

their business to make sure that their employer would not get away with this. They marshalled the labour force and ensured that at least forty or fifty men done their share of picketing every day. At first many of the lorry drivers were very hesitant about turning around and not going in to either collect or drop off their cargo. But as the days wore on the place was bottled up with practically no transport at all crossing our picket line which flushed out the shop steward for the men who worked in the container base. He had already been approached and given assurances that although we were claiming the work as ours we would also ensure that not one man would be made redundant as a result of our actions.

    The men working in Chobham Farm chose to ignore our offer and after telling the employers what we had said they then chose to join forces with the employers in trying to see us off. Now when they could see that we meant business the shop steward Tony Churchman met with us and once again we gave the same assurances only this time we offered the men inside the chance of a lifetime we asked them through their shop steward if they would come and join us on the picket line we would fight to get them a registration. This too was rejected and it emerged later that the men inside the container base were also in constant dialogue with the T & G paid officers. But it was clear to even the shortest sighted person on the planet that Chobham Farm was doomed. Unless they approached the dock officers with a view to employing registered labour they would go bust.

    Then private detectives appeared on the scene

handing out writs from John Donaldson's court like confetti at a wedding. They were issued to any shop steward who happened to be picketing once the men rumbled who they were they informed him that a particular man was a leading light in the shop stewards movement. The private detective then tried to serve the writ on this man who decided to go for a stroll and the detective followed him after about three miles the detective made a spurt and caught up with the man serving the writ.

The man burst out laughing and as he tore the writ up into little pieces he informed the now knackered detective that not only was he not a shop steward but he never worked in the docks. He was a relative of one of the pickets and the man had just popped down to see for himself what was going on.

The T.V and the media descended upon Chobham Farm when they realised that the place was about to crumble, our first victory was in sight and another container base at Barking applied to employ registered dockworkers. We could smell victory so much so that a group of our pickets visited another container base near Chobham Farm. This one was the apple tree in the orchid it was the London International Freight Terminal (commonly known as the LIFT) and we estimated that there was 1,200 jobs there. This was the one that would make or break our campaign for when we beat this group the rest would swallow and employ registered dockworkers.

But just as we were thinking of moving on to the next container base just leaving a token picket at Chobham Farm BANG the tip staff from the Industrial Relations court served three writs on our members. Unless they ceased picketing (two of them never picketed Chobham Farm) they would be arrested on that Friday and imprisoned for contempt. The three shop stewards named was the chairman of the shop stewards Vic Turner and the secretary Bernie Steers plus the one shop steward out of the three named who had indeed been picketing Alan Williams better known as Willie. It later occurred that he had been named as Tony Churchman the shop steward for the men in the container base had recognised Willie as he used to go to school with him!

Come Friday and the Port of London stopped work and there was a mass picket outside Chobham Farm. The time that the tipstaff and the police were due to make their arrest was 2 p.m. a ridiculous choice because that gave all our men all day to frequent the local public houses, and sure enough as two o'clock approached the mood got decidedly ugly and I don't think that the police had a cat in hells chance of picking up our men.

Taking into account that this container base was situated in a residential area the local people had never seen scenes like they were witnessing. There must have been some eight to ten thousand men demonstrating and despite the shop stewards pleas for no violence the men made their views known that no one was going to arrest their leaders- no matter what it took. Things looked very nasty.

Then the BBC radio presenter called us to one side and informed me that there had been developments at the court in Chancery Lane. He said that the Government had sent the official solicitor to represent the men and that with his intervention the writs had been withdrawn! Who the hell was the official solicitor? It turned out that he is able to intervene in cases were the accused are unable to represent themselves. This was normally because the accused was insane! The Government had certainly pulled a rabbit out of the hat.

So the Government had avoided a showdown that might have brought our problem to the surface and perhaps something positive might have come out of it. However we knew that our campaign had all the top guns reeling and the strength of the national port shop stewards was at an All-time high. The men knew that they could trust the leadership as the shop stewards held regular mass meetings and involved the men in the picketing and blacking of any transport firm that crossed our lines. This was the difference between an official dispute and unofficial action the powers to be could not approach individual leaders in an attempt to get the action called off whereas when the union lead the dispute telephone calls are made and secret deals are hatched in the best way to end the dispute.

However for the first time in the London port shop stewards a split was emerging as many of the younger shop stewards wanted to move the bar to a new height by picketing the LIFT container depot. They believed that they had secured the rights to make Chobham Farm and Barking containerbases employ registered labour and they thought that with the strength of the shop stewards movement they could knock over what was the biggest container base in South East England. For some unknown reason the leadership of the shop stewards movement showed their opposition to this and wanted to knock over some smaller container bases. Their opposition to picketing the LIFT did not go down to well with the younger shop stewards who had in the main done a large proportion of the work involved in getting Chobham Farm.

    The argument about where to go next rumbled on and at every London shop stewards meeting the subject was raised with the opponents still adamant that it would be better to go to the smaller depots. As the days wore on it was evident that the communist party members were behind the blocking of picketing the LIFT. At every meeting they blurted out the same old reasons why we should not do the LIFT and just concentrate on smaller depots. However something else was waiting that would eclipse everything.

    The London port shop stewards were holding a routine meeting at the Poplar and Blackwell rowing clubs hall on a Friday afternoon when Brian Nicholson came into the hall and asked if he could speak to us. Nicholson was chairman of the executive committee of the T & G and they don't come any more powerful than that, he never held high opinions of the unofficial committees and later it emerged that he was feeding M.I 5 with information about certain shop stewards and other information. However we never knew that at the time and he then dropped a bombshell by saying that five of our members would be arrested that day and taken to Pentonville prison for contempt of court. The court of course was the industrial relations court and they had issued writs against three men who were picketing Lord Vesteys Midland Cold storage depot in Leyton, East London also included on the writ was our chairman and secretary.

    That Friday afternoon would change all our plans. The priority would be to protect our members who were to be picked up by the old bill and carted off to Pentonville. We considered and discussed with those involved if they wanted to appear at the infamous court and agree with Donaldson that they would not picket Vesteys depot again. We told Tony Merrick, Connie Clancy and Derrick Watkins that there were plenty of others who would take their place on the picket lines and we then asked Vic Turner our chairman and Bernie Steers our secretary if they wanted to resign and also agree not to have any further dealings with Vesteys Midland Cold Storage depot. All five refused point blank.

    Vestey had got his directors at Midland Cold Storage to apply to the court to try and bring about an end to the picketing. Lo and behold four of our men were picked up that same afternoon and taken to Pentonville Prison. We then took a decision then that would remain in the annuls of trade union history that was to picket Pentonville prison until our members were released. We never knew how successful this would be but we knew our men would not take kindly to anyone imprisoning our members. It goes without saying that on that Friday afternoon a national dock strike commenced. Ports who had never attended the national port shop stewards meetings walked out to a man. The reason that only four out of the five had been picked was because our chairman Vic Turner decided to have a few beers at his local before going to jail!

The Daily Express seized upon this and proclaimed that the chairman who should be inside Pentonville with his mates had gone on the run. In fact Vic Turner was outside Pentonville prison with us picketing! Once the police had been informed who he was they duly arrested him and he never had far to go before being imprisoned! The Daily Express was the only national newspaper that was printed during the time that we had men in prison. Not only did they peddle out right wing filth but their workers scabbed and had to print the paper with police guarding them. The rest of Fleet Street had walked out however they needed a lot of persuading before they downed tools.

As I had covered the Pentonville affair in full in my first book, The Death of the Docks I asked another shop steward to give his account on how he saw what took place when the Government put our five men in prison.

The following account is the experiences of Tony Banfield a shop steward in London's Royal Docks. He was a shop steward at T. Wallis (Royal Docks) Ltd the very same company that had invested heavily in Chobham Farm. Tony had worked in the London Dock before being sent to the Royal Docks when all the wharves had been sold off to property speculators and venture capitalists.

It is impossible to begin my account of what took place for the time that our men were imprisoned without giving some personal background of how I arrived in the Royal Docks and participated in what many people in the working class movement describe as one of the greatest displays of what the working class can achieve when they stick together. This was a truly momentous moment that displayed everything good about workers and I can truly say that I was proud to be part of it. However it only came about through good leadership and plenty of hard work in organising everything.

At the end of the day everyone who became involved all had a common goal although many other sections of the working class while perhaps sharing the dockworkers struggle they knew that if the Government could knock over the dockworkers then the rest would be easy meat for them to decimate their industries.

Earlier in the book my Grand Father, William was mentioned as was my father George. This made me the third generation of my family to take up employment in the docks. We all worked in London Dock, Tooley Street to be precise. This covered areas such as Butlers Wharf right up to Canary Wharf. Given the location of our docks we could not load and unload the very big deep sea ocean going ships but we in the main traded with the Baltic and Scandinavian smaller ships that could navigate their way up to Tower Bridge and beyond. Also a lot of our work came in the shape of barges of meat that had been unloaded in the Royal Docks and the West India docks and it would then be brought to our wharves and we would unload it into a specialised cold storage wharf. We also handled much of the trade from the Canary Islands hence today all the rich people who live in Canary Wharf know that once the place was not all apartments and restaurant's but a place of work for many people.

Once the cargo had been unloaded into the warehouse's it would then be collected by Lorries and taken to wherever it was destined for on roads that had been constructed for horses and carts the method of transportation in the nineteenth and early twentieth century. The roads were and still are very narrow which caused a great deal of congestion right on the edge of the city of London. Another asset that the wharves provided was the fact that quite a large percentage of the work would also use the vast canal network that our country is blessed with yet is largely ignored in favour of using Lorries that not only clog up the roads but heavily pollute the atmosphere.

On leaving school at the ripe old age of fifteen my father took me along to his union branch meeting to register me and I duly joined the T & G. This practise was widespread as the industry depended on the father and son system to recruit labour for our industry. As the minimum age of entering the dock industry was twenty years of age I had to pursue other jobs while waiting for the National Dock Labour Board to send for me. What you had to appreciate was that recruitment only took place when the employers were short of labour and given that the old boys never had to retire as soon as they reached retirement age and that many of them had light duty jobs or that a gang would let an "oldun" remain in the gang and he would be given the easiest jobs.

So you couldn't automatically assume that once you reached twenty years of age that you would go straight into the docks. In fact where I worked there was a delivery gang of eight men who would take the cargo from the warehouse to the Lorries that had an average age of about seventy years! This was before the BBC thought of Dads Army!! But I say it with pride that we took it as part of our duty to look after our elders.

It wasn't long after my twentieth birthday that my brief came through. A brief was the dockology term for your registration book. I found it strange at first that no one called you by your name. As I was meeting with new people they would say oh your Georgie Banfields boy. Anyone who started in the docks had this to contend with after a few months people would gradually refer to me by my own name. Then you knew that you had been accepted.

I chose to try and get established at Wilsons Wharf and as such you had to attend the "call on" at 7.45 a.m. each morning to try and get a job should you either be late for the call or fail to get a job then you had to attend the pen or the box this was the name given to the national dock labour board offices were you would receive a bomper for that day and the pay for that was the princely sum of eleven shillings for a day's wages which in today's terms would be fifty five pence! I found the system to be very demeaning and as with most new recruits to the dock industry it took a while before you accepted this as part of the job. Given these working conditions things could really boil over at times but on the whole I thought that dockworkers behaved in a very dignified manner given the lot that they were faced with.

I spent the next eight years working there and on the whole it was very hard work but given the company you kept we just laughed it off. I was soon to discover that these men always viewed the half-filled glass as half full rather than half empty this speaks volumes for some of the toughest and hardest men that I have ever had the pleasure of working alongside. But as modernisation kicked in we were among the first to feel the effects of change. The wharves that made up the Pool of London plus any riverside wharf had become a hunting ground for property speculators who went under the name of asset strippers in the early 1960s.

This was not what the trade union had promised us when they introduced decasualisation they had banged on about dockworkers being given security of employment for the first time ever. They should have been nicked under the trade descriptions act! Lots of people got very rich on the backs of the dockworkers when they bought riverside wharfs and sold them on to developers. I only hope that the professional people today who own these upmarket riverside apartments sleep at night and are not haunted by the old dockworkers that they helped to sling them on the scrap heap.

Hays Wharf who were the main perpetrators of selling their riverside property had a massive twenty five acres of riverside property and rather than sell this premium land chose instead to lease it out. This of course was after they had fired all their dockworkers citing continuing losses left them with no other alternative. What a load of codswallop. They had already invested huge amounts of money in cold storage depots away from wharves and the docks. Not only did they do this but they played the sympathy card expecting people to feel sorry for them and they issued statements that they had tried in vain to make a go of it despite suffering enormous losses. No-one from the trade union asked them why they had not offered the dockworkers that they employed the chance to work at their new depots.

The Royal Group of Docks was my next port of call along with many more of the workforce that the wharf owners had dispensed with. We were only glad that the men in the Royal Docks accepted us and made us feel welcome. Being sent to another dock only came about as a result of the dock labour scheme which gave us protection from being sacked other than the usual misdemeanours of stealing or for fighting. For the men who had lost their livelihoods purely because of the location of the wharf that they worked the dock labour scheme was indeed a godsend. My new employer was Tom Wallis. Little did we know that he was just as unscrupulous as the employer that I had just left.

Although I had been working under the riverside agreement we too had been taken in by the statements regarding the decasualisation agreement a couple of years ago. The promise of security of employment seemed a million light years away in fact many of us thought that we were worse off since the introduction of the Devlin report however the men of the Royal Group of Docks made us welcome in our hour of need and I will always remember this as it showed many of us up who had questioned the militancy of the men of the Royal Docks.

The riverside agreement even after decasualisation

still gave the labour masters total control over as to who got the best jobs and who went to work. Firstly they picked up their regular workers who were their preferred labour. This was not unusual as the men knew the job back to front and this would be reflected in the output. Should the labour master have to employ men who were not familiar with the workings of the wharf then the output would dip sharply. But even allowing for this the labour masters knew the power that they held and many of them abused their position when engaging labour for their particular jobs.

The men who worked at the wharves where I worked showed plenty of patience and understanding considering that many of them had done the job for years and working flat out to achieve a high output came as a second nature to them. Given the fact that the men in the Royals had been out on strike in 1967 over the continuity rule for over six weeks and the men in the London Docks had refused to support them and now found themselves pitched in with a group of men who held no grudges. They knew that certain men in the London Docks had tried in vain to get the men to support the strike and it was to these men that the men of the Royals dropped any resentment or grudges.

As for me I soon found out that these men were highly educated in the ways of the world and I found it a privilege to work alongside a group of men who understood what was going on and never had the same view as many of the men with whom I had worked previously and where all they saw was no further than that week's wage packet and more importantly they didn't want to do anything that might harm or damage the employer that they worked for. Well when they found themselves on the scrapheap because the employers that they had served obediently for years had taken the golden shilling from the property developers and returned their entire labour force to the national dock labour board. What price loyalty now?

I was amazed at the way the labour was allocated to work when I arrived at Tommy Wallis's. The shop stewards oversaw every job which in turn ensured that all the better jobs were shared out evenly between the entire labour forces-the same rule applied for the not so good jobs to. Little did I know that on that very first day my whole life would change and I put that down to working alongside a group of men who perhaps lacked educational degrees or qualifications but most certainly held a degree when it came to the University of Life. They held conversations about containerisation or how the unions were failing to get to grips with the problems that our industry faced. In fact many of these men held a more sensible and balanced conversation than our M.Ps!

It would be wrong of me not to say that quite a few Royal Group dockworkers viewed us as scabs or tarries because of our chequered history in the past. However once the picketing started we threw ourselves whole heartedly into the campaign and a lot of our men had never experienced leadership like the shop stewards were giving. They made you feel important they praised you for picketing which gave you a sense of pride as someone appreciated what you were doing. The best way to get your men behind you is to involve them and hand out praise. I felt that we were really achieving something and it became a pleasure to work alongside the shop stewards.

I had never worked on such large ships as the ones that were berthed in the Royal Docks, in the pool of London you only ever got to work on ships that were called short sea traders, these smaller ships were designed to trade between the continent and the upper pool of London. Whereas in the Royal Docks I discovered that the ships were ocean going ships and as such they were huge alongside anything that we had previously worked.

In London Docks we usually worked the same cargoes from the same countries. Here you could walk along the dockside and each ship that was berthed had arrived from destinations from all parts of the world.

Another new concept to most of us was the size of the labour force. We had got used to working with the same gang of men week in week out but here you got to meet different people every day and it was this that I believe helped broaden your outlook with men who would debate almost everything giving you a different view on most things. But the one thing everyone agreed on was the growing threat that the container's posed and it was through this that I discovered what a tight knit community the dockworkers were.

We hardly had time to draw breath when the second phase of the modernisation agreement was being introduced which meant that a shift system was to be introduced. Although many of the men were against this it was eventually voted in. It turned out to be a blessing in disguise to me as by splitting the labour force into two shifts meant that more shop stewards' had to be elected.

Just before the elections I was approached by various men asking if I would consider standing.

My credentials stood me in good stead as my family had all been good trade unionists and had good names in the industry without which you stood no chance of being elected. I was duly elected and must admit that I felt very humble alongside some of my peers who had served the men for years and had built up a huge amount of trust with the men. I listened and learned from my fellow stewards and the first thing that I picked up on was that we were elected by the men and at all times we should strive to keep in touch with them and not remove ourselves from their struggles and the most important thing that I had rammed down my throat was that we should never allow ourselves to earn more money than what the men we represent earn.

This was solid gold advice as the employers were forever attempting to give us rewards such as putting the shop stewards on the highest paid job of the day. If the men had thought that we were on the highest paid jobs every day then the trust that had been built up would disappear faster than the Titanic sunk. The employers knew this and they were forever trying to woo the shop stewards with extra payments all of which I am glad to say was never ever accepted.

The London port shop stewards committee was now meeting two or three times a week to discuss the ever growing problem of the containerbases that were springing up everywhere. In fact such was the cheek of the road hauliers a company called Woodcocks started to operate groupage work just a couple of hundred yards from the Royal Albert Dock in London. Although I had only just started attending these meetings I quickly discovered that many of the shop stewards were full of anger towards the union's inability to support our claim to the container base work. It was universally agreed that the only way we could tackle the problem was by going national and that meant making contact with shop stewards in every major port.

Shop stewards travelled to every major port in an effort to bring about a national port shop stewards movement. All this cost money in travelling expenses but true to form just as the working classes had done over the years they put their hands in their pockets and gladly threw money into collection buckets. All this was done at mass meetings which were held on a regular basis. So after a few meetings of the national port shop stewards it was agreed that we would meet in Birmingham on Saturdays rather than in London or Liverpool. This was central and would reduce the travelling for everyone.

At first the meetings were dominated by London and Liverpool with Hull, Preston, Southampton and Glasgow joining in. In the beginning when shop stewards had to travel to ports it would sometimes involve an overnight stay needless to say they never checked into five star hotels like many of the trade union officials and politicians do but instead they would lodge at a fellow shop stewards home, sometimes just dossing down on the floor. In fact I put up a Liverpool shop steward when they travelled down to London. His name was Tony Burke a good man and the bond of friendship that developed from that struggle carried right on up to this very day.

As we began to grow stronger I was getting somewhat alarmed that the London shop stewards committee was forging itself into three influences. Firstly you had trade union delegates who were unpaid but gave up huge amounts of their time in attending union meetings in a vain attempt to get the unions physically involved in the struggle to get our work back.

These men could be branch secretaries or delegates in both unions they knew that whether you were a stevedore or a docker containerisation spelt the death knell for you. Many of these belonged to the Labour Party. Their devotion to help the working classes went without any rewards or adulations they were just ordinary working class people whose only objective was to better the lot of the people they represented.

Then you had the shop stewards who belonged to the far left political parties who spent far too much time attacking each other or trying to score a point over their political rivals. The third group of which I belonged to was the stewards who had no political affiliations whatsoever but the main goal was to get the trade unions to do their job properly failing this they would then take up the battle themselves. All of these groups were shooting into the same goal but sometimes because of outside influences they would want to take a far slower route to the goal. Then you had to ask the question of trade union delegates who sat on the unofficial shop stewards committee was it right for them to wear two hats?

Overall we were very well organised and every step

of the way in arriving at our decision to black and picket certain container depots was always done democratically. In fact at the company were I worked, Tommy Wallis we attended the amenity blocks during the meal breaks to give regular up to date reports and when the need arose for a mass meeting we held it between the two shifts. So the employer's idea of splitting the labour force into two halves with the hope that the men would lose any militancy had severely backfired on them.

    I saw my role as a foot soldier as I was certainly not a leading light by any means however I like many other so-called foot soldiers travelled the country to attend meetings and always being allowed to contribute in discussions before any new policy was formulated. At first this committee was almost totally ignored by the unions they saw it as a pressure group that would die out.

    That was until we came up with the policy of blacking and picketing certain container depots around every port that was affiliated to the national port shop stewards. Then when the union (T&G) informed us that Tommy Wallis and the Ben Line who were the two shareholders of the company where we worked had container base depots employing non registered labour, I found it rather strange that the union (T&G) knowing what was going on and that the workers there belonged to the T&G didn't do something themselves rather than hand a loaded gun to us to do their dirty work.

    The two container depots that our employers had invested huge sums of money into was London East (I.C.D), the I.C.D representing inland clearance depot, this was based in Stratford a mere bus ride from the docks. The other container depot was Barking container base which was part of the huge O.C.L group. This group was for the big boys of the shipping world and they had containerbases up and down the country. But both of these were owned or part owned by our employers who had sunk money into these ventures- money that the men who they were about to discard had helped them to make.

Anyhow it was now agreed at the national shop stewards meeting that we would nominate a couple of container base depots in each port and begin picketing them and any lorry that took cargo in or brought cargo out and had crossed our picket line in doing so would then be put on a list blacking that haulage firm nationally. In short if they wanted to run our picket line then they would not be able to get loaded or unloaded in any of the big ports. The only way that the company could be removed from that list was a letter from a director of that company giving an undertaking that their company would honour any of our picket lines.

As it began to bite the unions became agitated that we were undermining them and then the Government started to get involved. When all this started to happen we knew that we were on the right path and that we were hurting them. As many M.Ps and their peers in the House of Lords had investments in many of these ventures they began to sit up and take notice. Of course we never expected any plaudits from these people in fact they all joined forces and began attacking us calling us bully boys who were trying to replace fellow workers in the depots that the pickets had descended on. The Prime Minister even joined in by stating that the bully boys had descended upon an innocent cold storage depot in Leyton demanding that he employs dockworkers.

What Ted Heath forgot to mention was that the owner of that cold storage depot was our old mate Lord Vestey who figures very high in the rich list but not so high in paying any income tax on his vast fortunes. In fact for one financial year Vestey paid ten pence tax for the whole year! Explain that one away. But as the heat was being turned up certain shop stewards who held positions in the unions and also on the shop stewards committee had to decide what hat they wanted to wear. It was make your mind up time.

We all knew that the struggle was going to be a long and bitter dispute but this was going to be the last chance saloon if registered dockworkers were to have a future. As far as we were concerned this was it, no room for the fainthearted this was going to be a dispute to end them all. Although our strength had been considerably weakened by the introduction of containerisation and the never ending offers of severance pay to our men we still held the whip hand as the ship-owners and the port employers had not completed the modernisation programme. What had become apparent once word got out what the shop stewards proposed doing was that the leadership of the unions and that includes senior delegates who were dockworkers sitting on high powered committees stating their opposition to us taking action!

These people included the two dockworkers who sat

on the national executive committee of the T & G they represented the dockworkers on what was one of the most powerful committees in this country. Their names were Billy Powell and Brian Nicholson who was later named in cabinet papers as working for M.I 5. This wants some believing that a dockworker was feeding information to the M.I 5 on certain individual's political beliefs and who were the ring leaders!

 I suppose he thought that this was the best way to represent the dockworkers. Word had it that certain dock delegates from London docks received a payoff from one wharf and ensured that they went to another wharf who they thought was soon to close thereby getting further payoffs. These became known as the bounty hunters. This was no way to represent dockworkers they like many others had fallen into the trap of believing that what they were doing wasn't out of order. Well let me assure you it certainly was not in order.

 The blacking and picketing campaign was now well under way and it was Chobham Farm that was near to collapse purely due to the men at Tommy Wallis who once they had finished their shift descended upon the place to picket it. This was carefully organised by the shop stewards at Tommy Wallis's who arranged rotas so that everyone did their fair share of picketing. The press and the television descended upon the place and given the publicity that they gave to the place this only increased the amount of people who wanted to be seen to be picketing.

 As a shop steward I along with the other shop stewards wanted to lead by example and this meant putting in twelve to fifteen hours every day. Apart from doing your work we then dashed to Chobham Farm or had to attend meetings it was a whirlwind but an experience I never once regretted. But as things really hotted up some of our pickets reported that a few lorry drivers had taken to driving right through the picket line and not even slowing down. This could have killed or badly injured the men who were picketing and our policy of no violence was really being tested to the full. We informed our men that they had every right to protect themselves and I had the unfortunate experience of a lorry driver trying to drive through the picket line. He regretted that after he was stopped when he came out and he was given a right hander plus the fact his company was now blacked in nearly every port in the country.

    All in all the vast majority of lorry drivers behaved impeccably and we had very little trouble from them but I suppose the very few can always give their mates a bad name. But what probably brought most of them into line was the sheer speed that their company appeared on the blacklist, if a lorry ignored our pickets then a simple phone call to Scruttons shop stewards who were organising the blacklist and that was that. The shop stewards at Scruttons would then phone up the other ports and within an hour that companies lorries were blacked nationally. I might add at this point that most of the larger haulage companies who were organised and all the drivers belonged to a union behaved impeccably and supported us to the hilt once they had heard our case.

    Other groups started to rally round and offer us

support such the International Socialist Party who helped us in printing leaflets and giving us information that they thought might be of assistance. Also the print workers at Bryant Colour who without hesitation printed thousands of placards that became a symbol. Bryant Colour workers themselves were involved in a dispute and their help meant a lot to us.

At the beginning of the campaign we found ourselves running here and running there all we were short of was a broom up our back passage and we could have swept up as well! But some of the men who picketed day in day out and never looked for any gratitude one person who springs to mind as a stalwart in picketing Chobham Farm was a small thin and balding man who went by the name of "no go George" a man of very high principles. I also have fond memories of standing on the picket line with my father. I have no doubt that many other men had the same experience but for me it meant a lot as we were shoulder to shoulder in trying to fight for our livelihood's.

Whilst many of our men were picketing relentlessly day in day out there was another very small group of shop stewards to whom we referred them as Hollywood dockers. The only time they appeared on the picket lines was when the press and the television cameras were in attendance, as soon as they disappeared so did the Hollywood dockers stating that they had an urgent meeting to attend! When you read Animal Farm you can readily associate these stewards with the pigs!

As it began to bite and Chobham Farm had become seriously wounded and like any animal that is wounded they began to lash out. Firstly the employers there tried to get a fleet of unmarked lorries to meet up with their workers at the nearby Wanstead Flats where they could transfer the cargo. Unfortunately for them we had a steward who had impersonated a BBC reporter and had spoken with the managing director of Chobham Farm who told him of their plans to outfox the dockers and their shop stewards! When the Lorries arrived they were greeted by a huge contingent of pickets! So the employers who were now getting fed up in the docks with lorry after lorry being turned away tried a ploy of their own they used non-union labour to work a small ship that would be berthed along the River Crouch near Colchester. Again once our men heard of this they flew down there and someone let go of the ships mooring ropes while someone else set fire to the shed that contained wood that had been unloaded.

    We held regular update meetings with our men letting them know how their efforts were going, and sometimes these meetings resembled a cup final crowd seeing their team score the winning goal! Such was the optimism of how the struggle was going. By now the 5 men were in Pentonville Prison three had picketed Lord Vesteys Midland Cold Storage Depot in Leyton. Three of the men Watkins, Clancy and Merrick had picketed the depot on a regular basis whilst the other two Turner and Steers were only named on the writ because they were chairman and secretary of the shop stewards committee.

    Someone advised us that the Ben Line shipping company and other shipping companies were berthing their ships on the continent to avoid getting caught up in the trouble. They would then ship the cargo or the containers back to England via the Dover cross channel ferry. So it was quickly agreed that we send a delegation to these ports to explain our case and ask that they don't handle any ships that were bound for any of the ports that were in dispute. By know every port in the country had joined the strike. Even ports who did not belong to the national port shop stewards movement had walked out and other industries were joining the strike every day.

The four stewards who had undertaken to visit the continent were Mickey Fenn, Alan Williams, Tony Delaney and myself set out and we hadn't gone very far before boarding the ferry when we were surrounded by four custom officers who asked us to get out of the car. We had not even shown our passports at this stage when one of the customs officer said you're the four dockers going on a so called holiday? Someone had briefed them and it was obvious that we were being monitored by the secret services. Or did one of our own who later was named as an M.I 5 informer grass us up? We knew that we were in trouble and Tony Delaney told the customs officers that we wanted a witness before they searched our car.

They had to agree to this and we gave them plenty of abuse as the search revealed nothing. We left them with we are Dockworker's do you really think we are that F...ing silly so as you could plant something in the car. After searching the car and questioning us we were allowed to board the ferry but we knew that our every move was being closely watched.

We arrived in Calais that evening and were met by

some French port workers who knew we were coming. We were taken to what appeared to be a working man's club where we were asked for our I,Ds, we produced these and a letter from the political party that had arranged everything and only then were made to be made welcome. Then they offered us all the help and hospitality that they could offer us. All in all they were a great bunch of lads. We explained that both Calais and Boulogne was crucial in our attempt to stop the shipping companies trying to beat the strike and after they had heard our case they gave us every assurance that they would examine containers very closely and any container that had been unloaded in Antwerp or Rotterdam instead of its British port would be blacked. One strange footnote to our meeting with our French counterparts was that they advised us not to travel on the roads overnight as many of their leaders had met with mysterious accidents!

Our next port of call was Antwerp which at the time was Europe's largest container port. They never had shop stewards as we know them so we met with a trade union official who just like his counterparts over here was very anti towards much of what we had to say. I wondered if he had been informed in advance of us arriving. Onwards to Amsterdam. Where we were met and told to follow this car. It took us to an office on the outskirts in the centre of Amsterdam were we were told to leave our car parked and we were taken in one of their cars.

Again we explained our case and what these dockworkers could not understand was why the unions were not leading the struggle. We told them that we could not understand that either! What helped us was the fact that most of the people we met spoke perfect English which was just as well as none of us could speak a word of their language! The whole trip was very spooky and resembled something from a film showing how the French resistance acted in the war!

We had done our bit and we now set off for home wondering what was happening there. The people we had met had given us assurances that they would do their best to help us. You could not ask for more. We all agreed that it worth the effort that we had put in and it appeared from that day the Tory party and its press claimed the whole dispute was politically motivated. We knew that that's why we had five of our members in Pentonville Prison. I couldn't help wondering why the trade unions had never asked our brothers on the continent for assistance before. It seemed the logical thing to do and more importantly it would stop ship-owners playing one port against another.

When we returned and reported back to the shop stewards as to what we thought we had achieved we were delighted to hear that the Ben Line ships that had slipped into Antwerp had been blacked. This gave us a boost and it was a severe kick up the backside for both the union officials and the ship-owners. They now knew that we would go to any lengths to achieve our goals. If I thought that was that then I could never be more wrong. The shop stewards then organised five different groups to visit Fleet Street, factories bus garages underground workers and the representatives of the miners.

Most of these groups were already organising their

members to join the strike which was now growing at a rate that was worrying both the Government and the trade unions. It was out of control and the bit that was worrying them was they had no control whatsoever on the strike.

Outside Pentonville the crowds had grown to huge proportions and a march was planned for the Tuesday. Then word reached us that the T.U.C where calling a one day general strike. Ye gods what was happening? The House of Commons was holding a debate on what was going on (more like what was not going on). Outside Pentonville now there where miners, bus drivers, factory workers, construction workers, print workers, fringe groups and many more.

It was like a carnival and at night time after everyone had oiled their vocal chords with a few pints began to sing so that the prisoners could hear it. The publican who had the pub opposite the prison opened his window and bellowed out I am trying to get some sleep. The abuse he got would be unprintable. He never shouted about the money he was taking every day he needed someone to hose down the cash register where it was so hot through the constant ringing up for drinks!

I had never witnessed anything like this and I returned home to fetch my Son Neil who was only twelve at the time. I told him "look at all this son you are witnessing working class history, don't ever forget where you came from. These people are your kind and given this show of solidarity there is nothing that the working class cannot achieve" People thought I was mad taking a young lad to such a huge demonstration but as my son will testify that moment will remain with him for the rest of his life. His chosen profession is in a greedy world were money is thrown around like confetti but I am proud to say that he has remained and always will be a member of the working classes.

All of this wasn't without the dockland humour. One of hundreds of incidents shows when a march was taking place on the prison a bus driver whose bus had got caught up in the march started hurling abuse about dockworkers. When someone asked him why he wasn't out on strike with his workmates this really tipped him over the edge! F--- the dockers was his reply. What he never knew that while he was abusing us one of our lot was letting his tyres down. Four flat tyres I bet he thinks twice after that before abusing people!

Come the Tuesday our men had now been in prison for five days and a march on the prison had been planned. It set out from Hyde Park and such was the enormity of the demonstration that when the front of the march arrived at the prison people were still setting off from Hyde Park. I still believe that this ranks as one of the largest demonstrations that our capital has ever witnessed. This was when the miners announced that when they returned from their holidays the following Monday there would be a national strike in support of the five imprisoned dockworkers.

This was another own goal for the Government as they had carefully planned the arrest of our men to coincide with the annual close down of many large industries who always had their holidays on the last two weeks in July. The Government thought that this would stop any support from the mines, the car workers and other large industries that shut down for that period. Then when the General Council of the T.U.C announced that t was calling a one day general strike the game was up.

Someone visited the five men in prison and suggested that when they were wheeled into the Governor's office each morning to ask them if they were prepared to adhere to the Industrial Relations Courts decision that they agree not to picket the place and the chairman and secretary stand down. Then other people could carry on the fight ad it was suggested that they should agree not to carry on with their contempt of court which had led to their imprisonment. All they had to do was to agree to this and they would be freed. Our men turned it down flat.

Amongst all the chaos given the amount of people outside the prison and as usual it attracted all the looney groups that go with any demonstration however there was one small group who introduced themselves to us. It turned out that they were squatters and they had "acquired" a large house just around the corner from the prison. They told us that if we wanted something to eat or to have a snooze then the house was available at all times for us. Well I have to say that these people had wonderful intentions but one visit was enough as the place seemed like it was running alive with vermin also it was cooty and many of their guests seemed to have been boycotting soap for a long while!

The snack that they had prepared for us was a huge

pot of stew. Given that this was July and taking into account the surroundings they never had many takers! However we noticed that one of our lot had made himself at home and appeared to be having the time of his life it was no go George! He was as happy as a pig in shit! Good on yer George. Another of our lot was fast asleep on a settee it was Tony Delaney who when he woke up one of the squatters asked him if he was comfortable, he replied that the sleep had done him good and the squatter lady told him that they had found the settee on some waste ground and that she thought it was full of fleas!

    The following morning saw the Government run up the white flag it was announced that the five would be released from prison unconditionally. At ten o'clock jubilant scenes welcomed our men. They were carried shoulder high to the awaiting cars to let them meet with their loved ones and then onto a never ending round of meetings. We had won. Or had we? Our fight to get back our jobs had been overshadowed by this and things were about to take a very strange twist.

    In conclusion I must say that I was proud to have been part of the huge effort that saw our five men released from prison. I shall cherish the memories of those six days for as long as I live. The great tragedy is that the younger generation today no nothing of what struggles that we and our Fathers and their Fathers had to endure so as they got a better start in life than we did. They take everything for granted none of them are street wise they have been brought up in an environment where it is the norm that as long as I am alright then its o.k.

Be assured this is not the right way forward. Ask your mother or father or your grandparents what they had to endure in their early part of life and more importantly if you think your cosy little world is safe then think on because when the bosses are ready to change tack then you and your mates will find yourselves on the scrap heap. Don't think it won't happen to you and, as many of the younger generation do not belong to a trade union when it happens you are on your own.

My story does not have a happy ending as the divisions within the Royal Group of Docks shop stewards opened up over whether or not we should picket the LIFT container depot. Also the day after our men had been released from prison the T & G called an official national dock strike. This completely took over the whole situation and removed any control that the unofficial shop stewards had. It was all but over.

We had so much control over our own destiny and the future of our industry two weeks ago and now because of a reason not known to this day the communist party stopped us from picketing the largest container depot in South East England. The communist stewards made sure that we never won the vote and the split was incurable. It took us (the communist party stewards all jacked it in and became official delegates!) months to get over it and the younger element of the shop stewards had to pick up the pieces. But while this was happening we had lost the war that we had declared on the non-registered containerbases.

What really hurt me and all the men who had relentlessly given up their time to win jobs in Chobham

Farm and Barking Container base was that the dig white chiefs who never done a day's picketing were now running up the flag of surrender. This was our Waterloo and we had the taste of victory in our nostrils only to be denied the final onslaught. This would have saved our industry from oblivion. The same group of men worked tirelessly to ensure that our men were released from Pentonville and then the two leading lights that had been imprisoned then orchestrated a campaign not to picket the LIFT. This was done on orders from King Street the headquarters of the communist party.

    Then you had the union delegates and the members of the Labour Party who really believed that Jack Jones would deliver us jobs through his participation on the Aldington/Jones committee that had been set up to solve the crisis. Well can pigs really fly? All that committee ever did was to increase the amount of severance pay to get rid of Dockworkers. Finally there was a small number of socialist worker members who were also shop stewards these never flinched and as far as I am aware they voted in line with what they thought was the best for the men who elected them. A pity others never remembered who elected them! That was my friend Tony Banfields account of how he saw the events that led up to the imprisonment of five of our members for trying to get back work that was rightfully ours.

The Aftermath

So the Government had climbed down and released our men unconditionally. We were absolutely cock- a- hoop, we knew now that we could march onwards to any container base and knock them over. No container base was beyond our reach, we knew that if we carried on with our campaign the dock industry had a future. Little did we know what was waiting around the corner for us?

Before I write about post Pentonville I would like to write about some of the lighter moments that took place during the incarnation of our men. I was appointed to oversee the strike H.Q in Plaistow the local labour party had kindly let us have the run of their place. The shop stewards also placed me in charge of the picketing of Pentonville at night! This meant that I wouldn't be going home until our men were released. One of the first overseas delegations to arrive at the strike H.Q was a group of Swedish Students. They asked if some of our blokes could put them up. There was a mad scramble in offering accommodation to the two girls who were amongst their lot. There certainly was not a shortage of housing for these!

Then one night a fellow steward told me that

someone wanted to speak to me and that these two men would take me to her. The two men were built like brick shithouses and as they were taking me down to a deserted area I began to fear the worse. Then a woman dressed in combat clothes thrust her hand towards me to shake my hand. She then congratulated us on a fine turn out and then came out with a corker "you have the men and I can supply guns and weapons so as we can storm the prison and release your men" I realised she was deadly serious and given the presence of the two minders I thought that I was in trouble. I replied by thanking her for such a kind offer but told her that we wanted to get our men out by peaceful methods. She along with her two minders disappeared in an instant and I retired to the pub to recover. It turned out she was Dr Rose Dugdale an I.R.A sympathiser who came from a well to do family and later used the family's art collection to fund the I.R.A. She also helped in hiring a helicopter and flying over a police station and dropping bombs onto it! Quiet old life I thought!

    Then there was the time when I had finished my stint at the strike headquarters and was about to make my way to Pentonville by train when someone piped up with "Arthurs going that way jump in his car and he will give you a lift "So ever grateful of not having to mess about on the underground I duly got into Arthurs car. We had gone about half a mile when we were approaching a set of traffic lights which were on red and Arthur was showing no inclination of slowing down." Watch out for the lights Arthur" I said to which he replied "what lights" and proceeded to drive right through them!

It turned out he was Docklands answer to Colonel Blink he was as blind as a bat and had two sterilised milk bottles as glasses! I told him to pull over and I got a train to Pentonville.

On the night that our men were released we went out for a celebration drink with our wives and a good few of the national port shop stewards. As the evening wore on we decided to go back to my place and continue the drink. There was a national docks delegate conference the next day so it made sense to let everyone get their head down at my pace for a few hours before setting off for Transport House. My wife wasn't too pleased with me as we had only recently moved into this maisonette a few weeks earlier and we hadn't finished unpacking. Tea chests everywhere but good people take you as you are and take it from me these were good people.

The next morning we all met up at Transport House not expecting too much from the union who had called the conference to discuss the question of dock work! Jack Jones was to address the conference and we held out very little hope of anything being done. As was the norm all this wasn't without its usual dramas and the Liverpool stewards told us that they had been to the Dorchester Hotel for breakfast! One of our stewards Tony Delaney had ordered taxis and had taken them to the Dorchester. They had a grand breakfast buck's fizz and he even ordered button holes for everyone. When the moment of reckoning arrived and the bill was presented he calmly informed the waiter that they were dockworkers and that as they were on strike they had no money! The head waiter just asked them to leave quietly!

Then a bombshell was dropped the delegates had voted to call a national dock strike! The voting was overwhelmingly in favour. What this meant was the small ports who had only a few men all abstained leaving the voting to the major ports. So as our strike had ended with the release of our men another one commenced. Jack Jones told a packed press conference that this strike would not end until dockworkers got their rightful jobs back.

The Aldington/Jones committee was reconvened as a matter of urgency. Their track record hardly set you alight up to now they had not produced one single job. They had however been responsible for ridding the industry of thousands of men who had become surplus to requirement's as a result of containerisation! So had they got our work back then the need for severance pay would be pointless.

The Guardian reported the next day that some five hundred men had massed outside the conference and if the delegates valued their lives they would reject the proposals being recommended by the joint working party.

What the delegates had rejected was another reduction in the labour force strength with some people viewing the agreement as a form of compulsory redundancy for selected people over the age of 55. Again no jobs had been sought with the only mention of this in the agreement that the Port of London Authority would seek to get groupage work into the docks.

So we now had a national dock strike which may

have been a few years late but this was it as far as we were concerned. This was do or die. The realist amongst us knew in our hearts that the union would sell us out so it was back to business for us. We called for a meeting of the London shop stewards to evaluate what we had achieved and what our next move would be. We were still buzzing from our victories at Chobham Farm and Barking container base not to mention getting the five men released from prison.

    We couldn't do too much while there was a national strike on as we had very little contact with our men and without them and without their endorsement of any further actions we would never had been able to maintain a strong picket line. The few of us who were still willing and available just kept up the picketing at Vesteys Midland Cold Store, and at Hays Transport groupage depot in Dagenham. The Government declared a state of emergency after the strike was a few days old. This was the norm as the Government had to cover its back in case things really went badly wrong for them. The Joint committee met every day in trying to thrash out a deal that would be acceptable to the delegates. I must say that at this point the men had not been consulted once by the unions as to what was happening and what they were striving to achieve.

    We knew the old adage of the unions taking over a dispute now had control of the situation whereas before when the unofficial shop stewards were running the show the unions had virtually no say in how the dispute should be run. Then ten days after the strike had been called the union reconvened the delegates to consider fresh proposals.

The so called "fresh" proposals should have been taken to the trade descriptions offices. The signatories would have been thrown in jail for misleading and telling utter lies to an entire industry. The Jones/Aldington report once again delivered no work for us and stated that this was in fact a very hard ask. They then came up with a piece of pure magic that Tommy Cooper would have been proud of.

They proposed that every container that had been loaded by non-registered labour should carry a levy. As to where this levy would go no-one knew. Severance pay was to be increased and the dreaded unattached pool was to be abolished. If the delegates had examined the offer closely then they would have rejected it out of hand as the unattached pool shouldn't have been allowed to be resurrected again.

Making that as the cornerstone of the offer was the equivalent of a bully who has been beating up a person every day agreeing that he will stop. Big deal! As for increasing the severance pay this was what the shop stewards campaign was against. By continually reducing the size of the register they were draining the blood out of our industry. We wanted an assurance that containerbases would be brought into the dock labour scheme. This was the sell-out of all sell outs.

When the news broke that the small ports who employed small amounts of people had voted the deal through all hell broke out. The union had got the small ports to accept the deal and not only had the union taken over the dispute that we were running very successfully but they had now weakened our position by calling a strike that had achieved nothing.

Jack Jones to his credit saw the bitterness and anger that the men were displaying so he threw open the large conference room to meet with the men. He tried in vain to explain away what he had done but he was fighting a losing battle and when someone aimed a large brass ashtray at him we knew that it was time to call a halt to this. The ashtray had missed him by a whisker and had it hit him it would have taken his head off! Give him his do Jack Jones never flinched and tried to carry on selling the deal that he had sold to some of the delegates.

The London shop stewards also were in a mess with divisions that would prove to be fatal. The communist party had pulled out all the stops to prevent us picketing the L.I.F.T every time we had a vote the chairman would put it back to the next meeting giving the opponents of any such actions a chance to get shop stewards who did not usually attend meetings to vote against us.

We held a mas meeting of the men to recommend that we continued with the strike but before our meeting was held news just got worse and worse with port after port voting to go back to work. We considered revising our recommendation but decided to put it to the men and lo and behold they voted overwhelmingly to return to work.

The union had done us this was our last fight and we were winning it hands down before the union took over and sold us out. To make matters worse all the leading lights of the Royal Docks shop stewards resigned- it was just a coincidence that they were communist party members or sympathiser's. They walked away letting the men know and many of them took up positions within the union! After what they had done to us!

This left the shop stewards in total disarray and as the men were aware of the split it was hardly likely that they would agree to enter another campaign and as the mood was as black as coal many more men were taking the easy option by applying for the severance pay.

The "new" shop stewards committee held a few mass meetings to let the men know that we were still active and that more importantly we were there for them. Many of our former colleagues had taken up their new posts in the union. What they expected to achieve to this day I am at a loss if they thought that the men would give them the same respect as they had enjoyed being on the shop stewards committee well they must have been on something!

Respect doesn't just grow on trees nor does it just happen you earn the trust of your men and without respect you are going nowhere. Too many people think that they can get themselves elected and hey presto when it suits them they turn to the men. When the men hesitate in giving them support they are shocked. Most of those who had walked away from the unofficial shop stewards movement were of the older generation of dockworkers leaving the younger generation to whom they called the school children.

Well the so called school children had done most of the leg work, attended meetings regularly and most importantly to the men they had been on the picket line day after day. Anyone can sit in their ivory tower giving out orders. Gradually the men began to attend the meetings again but they knew that the war had been lost.

The shop stewards who had mysteriously become born again Christians by going all official after all that they had witnessed in seeing how the unions had sold us out. They seemed to be content with their semi-retired life inside the union. If they really believed that they could change the course of events then both they and the communist party needed to book into a rehab clinic for down and out dockworkers!

What really got us back on the road and involved our men again was the sudden closure of the not so good Lord Vesteys operations in London. Less than a year after he had been responsible for imprisoning five of our members he announced that his stevedoring company in London's Royal Docks was to cease trading in 1973. He employed over five hundred men and they were to be returned to the unattached pool.

This would have seen the men's wages plummet to less than half of what they received before the closure was announced. The shop stewards visited Jack Jones and asked him if this was what he had promised our members when selling the second phase of the modernisation agreement. Also we asked him what was going to happen to these men. He huffed and he puffed stating that dealing with ship-owners wasn't always easy! We reminded him of his promises that both he and the London port employers had made in guaranteeing that the unattached pool would never be resurrected again. At this point he said "instead of slagging me of at the mass meetings you should try and negotiate with the likes of Vestey"!

We told him that anytime that he wanted to arrange a meeting we would be only too happy to attend. Hey Presto a couple of days later I was summoned to the union office to be told that a meeting had been organised for that Wednesday with the employers and given that the men were due to be sacked that Friday there was not a great deal of breathing space.

I attended the World Trade Centre that Wednesday and the line up on the employer's side looked like a who's who from the city gentry. Lord Aldington, Sir John Page, Sir John Cuckney who would later become a Baron and had been a leading spy for M.I 5 (he must have felt at home given the presence of a certain trade union delegate), then there was the star turn Lord Vestey added to these there was a couple more well-heeled employers. All in all there wasn't a day's work between the lot of them.

Jack Jones opened for the trade unions expressing deep concerns about Vesteys company closing on Friday to which Aldington responded that the company was yet another victim of containerisation and that the company had struggled on despite incurring heavy losses! Several more trade union delegates put in their contributions with the employers replying. We were getting absolutely nowhere fast it was like a mutual admiration society. Still Vestey had not spoken and after a couple of hours Lord

Aldington tried to close the gathering by announcing that despite everyone's efforts we should agree to disagree.

I had patiently sat and listened to the so called senior delegates and negotiators try and get a settlement. There was more chance of finding a pork chop in a synagogue than of this lot sorting out our problems. When you heard them perform you understood why our industry was in such a mess. I caught Lord Aldington's eye and he invited me to make a contribution.

I started off by attacking Lord Vestey for sacking over five hundred men while opening up cold store depots outside the docks. I also told them that it was not a case of agreeing to disagree as we were responsible for the very future of five hundred men's wage packet next week and that if we had to stay here all night to get an agreement then so be it. Lord Aldington looked visibly shocked and he began his reply by defending his colleague Lord Vestey and deplored the personal attack on him he then went on trying to be clever and asked "how would you solve this problem Mr Ross?" Thinking he was being clever. I told him that Vestey should make up the difference in the men's pay until they could be sent to a new employer.

Then very calmly I informed them that failure to get a settlement that was satisfactory to the men there would be a national dock strike commencing next Monday led by the national port shop stewards committee. Well this went down well! Lord Aldington asked for a recess but he did say that while he disagreed with everything that I had said and what I stood for I was very honest!

During the recess Jack Jones said that I had shown

him up! This really takes the biscuit. I told him he had done a good job himself in showing himself up. Anyhow when we went back the employers had a distinct change of heart and all the men would be allocated new employers. What it had proved was that even at the highest level the employers had buttered up the union reps. and they were treated as friends rather than the opposition. Shortly after that I was offered a job by Jack Jones to become a trade union paid officer. The very high powered delegate he used as a messenger couldn't believe that anyone would turn down such an offer. I had seen them and I wasn't going to play their game.

The men knew that it was the shop stewards who had pulled the rabbit out of the hat and we were once again the flavour of the month with them. The next chapter of us rebuilding the trust would be the coal miner's dispute in February 1974.

The Tory Government led by Ted Heath decided to take them on. Before long the whole country was on a three day week this was something that Hitler had failed to do! We organised our men to contribute every week and we took the money every Friday night down to the coal pit at Deal in Kent. The hospitality that the miners showed to us was too much to take!

They had their own social club and when word had got around who we were and when the president got up on the stage to announce us the drinks were coming at us in every direction. I only made the one trip-the hangover saw to that! Great people and when Thatcher organised her revenge mission in 1984 which led to a humiliating defeat for the miners after a year on strike no-one was now safe.

But our men were now once again firmly with the shop stewards and the national port shop stewards was again up and running. Without us knowing the T & G union were getting alarmed at the re-emergence of this group. What happened next can only add to the catastrophic mess that the union had put our industry in.

The Docks group committee that represented all dockworkers in South East England had realised that the shop stewards committee were once again rising up and although the industry had been severely weakened by the ever increasing severance pay they were once again taking action's that this time the union dare not ignore.

The shop stewards had once again come together less the communist party members who had by now taken up their posts as union delegates. The London docks group committee whose chairman was now Brian Nicholson called everyone out on strike over the definition of dock work and the job losses that the containerisation programme had brought about.

What Nicholson and his cronies had done was to call out London Dockworkers on their own. This was sheer madness and no-one believed that the strike would last more than a few days. How wrong everyone was! The very people who were running the strike had the means to get national support. When everyone realised that London had been thrown to the wolves by this committee it was too late.

Nicholson and his colleague's may have been good at getting the men out on strike but when it came to travelling to other ports for support the volunteers were thin on the ground. Far to many chiefs and nowhere near enough Indians. However the strike lasted for some five weeks and once again the last chance that we had in taking proper industrial action to try and get our work back had all but disappeared now.

Not only had this union committee left London isolated in trying to get our work back but the effect it had on the countries imports and exports was almost nil. After a few days nothing was in the papers or on the television news about the strike. What Nicholson was up to was to get support for the forthcoming bill that the Labour Government was about to introduce to extend the dock labour scheme to include all the non-scheme ports.

All the five week strike achieved was to alienate many people and the bill was eventually voted down with two labour M.Ps voting with the Tories which defeated the bill. This was game set and match for the dock industry. To this very day it is hard to work out the logic that was behind the strike. What makes matters even worse was the fact that many of the committee who were behind the strike had held their jobs for years and had continually failed to do anything when they held the key to solving our industries problems in the mid to late sixties.

Our industry was in steep decline and the people charged with looking after our interests had messed up big time and they now retreated back into their cosy little set ups and as the conventional work continued to disappear their solution was to take the easy option by gradually increasing the severance pay. This most certainly was not the answer. The Royal Docks was now the last survivor in London and that was marking time.

We had seen the disappearance of the upper pool and all the surrounding wharfs, and then we had the closures of the Surrey Commercial Docks, The East India Docks, The West India and Millwall Docks plus all the wharfs that flanked these docks. Added to this was the closure of Southern Stevedoring and Thames Stevedoring in the Royals. These two companies alone once employed over two thousand men. For the rest of us it was now only a matter of time.

Then out of the blue I turned up for work on a Wednesday afternoon when the superintendent asked me to go to his office as the owner Tom Wallis wanted a word with me on the phone. He calmly informed me that it was all over as the receiver was in he then asked me to thank the men for all their service! This man had no shame whatsoever!

Not only was it all over but all our men had done three days' work and under the terms of the insolvency no-one would receive a penny. I attended a meeting of the creditors and asked the receiver as to where all the fork lift trucks and other machinery had gone where upon I was informed that they had been sold for a paltry sum to the owners other company. This was who we were dealing with. Some months later we all received a cheque that gave us about two pence in the pound. Wallis owed me over forty pounds and my cheque was for eighty pence. Nice bloke.

As if this wasn't bad enough we were returned to the

pool where once again our wages plunged. The shop stewards called a meeting of all the men in the Royal Docks asking for their support but by now the fear of more redundancies had the remaining men frightened out of their lives.

They chose to carry on working believing if they struck in support of us their jobs would go. The irony of it was that it wasn't too long before they found themselves in the same boat. In the meantime the dock labour board allocated us all to new employers. After the men had turned their backs on us and refused to support us I made a promise to my wife that I would never again get involved to the extent that I had done so for fifteen years. I had given the men my all and when the moment came for them to return a little they chose the easy route.

I found myself along with six other men at Purfleet Deep Wharf, a riverside wharf in Purfleet, Essex who unloaded thousands upon thousands of tons of newsprint some by conventional methods, while much of it was unloaded on their roll on roll off berth. The managing director Derek Allison who was also chairman of the London Dock Labour Board greeted us on our first morning.

Whilst welcoming us he made it perfectly clear that the other six men were welcome but as far as I was concerned he made it clear that the company would be returning me to the local dock labour board at the earliest opportunity. Nice to be wanted.

He went on to explain that it wasn't personal but I came with a bad reputation and that everyone who worked at the wharf where part of one big happy family! I have heard that a few times. I thanked him and told him that whilst I wasn't being personal I had no intentions of letting him return me to the pool. This was a fatal mistake on my part for the next twelve months of my life were probably the most miserable twelve months of my life.

Purfleet Deep Wharf was just about the highest paid job in the docks anywhere. I think our weekly pay had been about £42 per week in the enclosed docks and my first weeks wage packet at Purfleet was over £300! However the men where the greediest people on this planet and most of them seemed to enjoy working while the rest of the docks where on strike.

The men also made it clear that they did not want me there and by all accounts the shop steward had held a meeting of the men who voted not to accept me. In hindsight I wish that I had gone to Tilbury where most of our men had gone. But I later found out that the men at Tilbury whilst not as hostile as the men at Purfleet viewed the shop stewards from the Royals as trouble makers and they were never really accepted.

The irony of all of this was that most of these men had started their working days in the Royal Docks or the West India docks. Strange how a pound note changes people. To illustrate how bad the men at Purfleet where the shop steward called a meeting about a ship that was to come on the roll on roll off berth over the bank holiday weekend. The ship had to work an all-nighter on the Sunday which would give you some £150 for the day's work.

Now every man at that wharf had earned best part of £300 each that week and here they were fighting and arguing over who was to get the Sunday job! I knew the game was up and I made my last speech slagging them off. But these people were beyond being shamed. I went home and told my good lady that I was finished. She told me that I had lasted longer than she thought and that I had been miserable for some months.

I put in my severance application over the weekend and believe this or not on the Tuesday Derek Allison came aboard the ship I was working on and called me up out of the ships hold. He told me that I was being let go that Friday! I wonder if all the men had the treatment of being waved goodbye by the managing director.

So came to an end of my life as a docker. I can put my hand on my heart and say that I tried my best along with some other good people to better the wretched conditions that our men had to endure, we tried to secure a future for our children to carry on the tradition of working in the docks as our fathers and their fathers did. I am not alone in stating that I was honoured to have represented some of the finest men that any industry had seen.

Soon another firm in the Royal Docks bit the dust. This time it was the largest independent employer Scruttons Maltby. That only speeded up the end of the Royal Docks. The P.L.A announced the closure of the Royal Group of Docks. All their labour force would be absorbed in Tilbury.

The men at Tilbury now saw that their dock and with

it their future was for the first time in jeopardy because of the size of the labour force. The severance pay had continually been increased to reduce the size of the register. This had not been in our game plan but it was most certainly in the port employer's game plan.

These people plan years ahead of what they plan on doing and they now had reduced the size of the labour force to what they had planned and they had also now got rid of the hot spot that being the Royal Docks. It was there that the employers met with the most resistance.

The men there seemed to be a different breed they stood up to the employers and had the union backed them they would still be working there today.

The Last Rites

This book has covered some bad people in the eyes of dockworkers starting way back in 1889 with Lord Devonport, then we had Churchill and keeping up the tradition of the Robber Barons along come Lord Vestey. These and many more like them kept up the tradition that anyone who worked in the docks should be treated as shit on the soles of their boots.

It was 1972 before a dockworker was able to have a cup of tea in a canteen where he worked. Also it was the same year that toilets that never stunk of stale urine and other unpleasant smells were built.

It was the same period before the men had asbestos put into sealed containers to prevent any further death and destruction that asbestos had caused for almost a hundred years. Even then when the men refused to unload it in hessian bags the employers moaned that more trade would be lost!

It took almost a hundred years before the employers rid the industry of the causal system and all the terrible things that came with it.

The employers had for a hundred years been

allowed to carry a few thousand men surplus. As the wages were so paltry they could afford to do this and with it came the fighting to get a day's work on the call. There was never a sorrier sight to be seen when grown men fought for some work. In the 1900s it could have been an hour's work!

The call on system was retained right up to 1967 despite successive Governments asking the port employer's to end it.

Then when they did deliver acceptable wages and working conditions they had already begun to open up container bases outside the dock with in the main non-union labour doing what would normally be done by dockworkers in the sheds and on the quay sides.

But in keeping with tradition you keep the best to last. Along comes Margaret Hilda Thatcher. The Tory party had been party to all the bad things that their chums the port employers had been doing in the docks for years and years. But- they had never dared to end the dock labour scheme.

They had secret reports as to whether they could end the scheme but every report come up with one similarity that was the men and the unofficial committees were to strong and would never allow the removal of their registration.

However much had changed, the severance pay had taken so many men out of the industry and many of them where men from the royals who did not want to travel to Tilbury to work. What made matters worse for the men was the fact that many of these men always supported the unofficial committees.

The labour force had been weakened to a point where Prime Minister Thatcher was ready to pounce. Another major casualty of the greatly reduced labour was the Blue Union their membership could no longer support the running of the union. This union had more history than the T & G; they were more in touch with their members than the T & G after the T & G got them expelled from the T.U.C in the fifties the relationship was an acrimonious one.

Jack Jones became the peacemaker between the two unions and in 1982 the Blue Union merged with the T & G. I still think that in hindsight every dockworker should have left the T & G and joined the Blue Union. Had they had more bargaining strength I believe there may have been a different outcome. Still hindsight was always a wonderful thing.

To those who think that I attack people for the sake of it let me assure you I only damn those who have wronged us. I only damn those who take jobs representing the workers and end up lining their own pockets. The darling of the left in the Labour Party was John Prescott (not my idea of a decent person at all). When the Tories were preparing the ground to abolish the dock labour scheme a meeting took place and the following is taken from a transcript.

The following article was by a Telegraph Journalist by the name of Iain Dale. He also worked for the National Association of Port Employers. He was given the task of clearing the decks ready for the abolition of the dock labour scheme.

He and Nicholas Finney the chairman of the port employers set about clearing the decks ready for the announcement that the scheme was to be abolished. They met with conservative M.Ps who of course were all in favour of it however, you would have expected a backlash from the Labour M.Ps especially the so called lefties.

When the two employer's representatives met with John Prescott and Michael Meacher this was part of their response to the news that Norman Fowler was going to announce that the scheme was to be repealed. Prescott who was the shadow transport secretary said "while we cannot be seen to support you publicly we will not lift a finger to support the unions when they try and get the bill defeated" The two turn coats added that they would have to go through the motions and make sceptical remarks.

This was the filth that purported to be on the side of the workers. Their argument (if they ever had one) was that dockworkers had a job for life; well if they cared to walk next door to the House of Lords they would see a house full of non-elected people who have a job for life.

By now Ron Todd was General Secretary of the T & G and as soon as the news broke that the scheme was to be abolished wildcat strikes broke out up and down the country. Two things to remember about this issue firstly it was the dockworkers and their money that founded the T & G and secondly when Bevan got the dockworkers their registration it had taken over fifty years of hard struggle to achieve it and that it was the jewel in the crown for every dockworker.

The registration prevented rogue employers (and we had plenty of them) from sacking people at will. You could still be sacked for a whole range of things such as fighting, thieving and many other things so why the urgency to get rid of the scheme. You may know that people in both houses of corruption don't get sacked for these and many more serious wrong doings. One of the loudest critics who was against the dockworkers was big Cyril Smith. Need I say any more?

The employers association commissioned a study by an economic group known as WEFA. They surprisingly came to the conclusion that by getting rid of the scheme would create some 48,000 jobs! What they meant was by closing down many of the ports this would release large areas of land that could then be turned into very nice riverside homes for the very rich people!

Then in a written answer to a question in Parliament on April 6th 1989 Norman Fowler the Secretary of State for Employment announced the Government's intention to repeal the Dock Labour scheme. If you want to know the true meaning of hypocrisy then you should see who jumped up on behalf of the opposition it was none other than Michael Meacher.

He accused the Government of wilful sabotage and that employers in many scheme ports were investing money in container schemes adding that the Government would be responsible for throwing the country into an economic mess that would follow after the dockworkers nationally would walk out on strike! This was the same man who met with employer's representatives assuring them that he would not hinder any progress in abolishing the scheme!

Something else that happened whilst all this was going on was that the intention to abolish the scheme had been leaked. This was what had prompted thousands of dockworkers up and down the country to walk out; it also forced the T & G into holding the strike ballot which had produced a vote in favour of industrial action.

It was claimed that both Margaret Thatcher and the shipping companies had been against the move to abolish the scheme. However, when the national association of port employers had revealed that they had "done their homework." Adding that they had covered every eventuality they went along with it. Then Ron Todd's bottle went.

He claimed that he had been advised by the unions legal section that as they would be striking against the Government an official strike could be viewed political. So it was off to the courts again. The Government and the employers had planned this to perfection because while the case was going from court to court the bill to abolish the scheme was making progress in Parliament and on July the 6th the bill received royal assent and that my friends was that.

The T & G had failed miserably to show leadership and men who were on strike heard that now the scheme had ended this would put their jobs on the line. People began to go back to work but then the employers sent out letters to anyone who they thought was a "troublemaker" informing them that they were sacked and enclosed a cheque for forty thousand pounds. Once again the T & G failed to get a grip and call out all its members. Ron Todd was now taking the employers to the arbitration committee for unfair dismissal.

It again beggars belief that the union never lashed out in response. Other men who had not been sacked were told if they never signed the new contracts they would be making themselves redundant. So we had sacked men picketing the dock gates while others who may be family or best friends having to cross the picket line!

The employment tribunal ruled that the men had been unfairly dismissed and ruled that the men should be reinstated. The employers refused to adhere to the tribunals findings so it was off to the courts again. Surely Ron Todd should have moved now. The union had now got the men on the back foot because the courts would now rule against the employers and make a further monetary award.

This duly took place and much to the shame of the union they had sold the dockworkers registrations for a cash cheque. This could not have happened in the States or in France. The press had a field day shouting that the jobs for life guarantee had finally gone.

Not one newspaper condemned the employers for setting up shop outside the docks to load and unload containers. Had the employers set up shop within the confines of the docks or even employed the labour that they had used for over a hundred years in the container bases that had sprung up outside every port in the country then there would still be a job for the registered dockworkers.

For those who the employers kept on the working conditions soon changed. Not for the better. All the fighting and sacrifices that had been made ever since Ben Tillet got the dockworkers their famous tanner had just been sold for a cash cheque.

You may think after reading this that the dockworkers got what they deserved. But I will leave you to consider this. It took the dockworkers over a hundred years before they finally got a decent basic wage and working conditions but within fifteen years they had nothing. I hope that you will have by now realised what bastards the port employers where. They only got away with abolishing the scheme with the help of the conservative party, two faced labour politician's and the transport unions failure to defend their members rights.

Printed in Great Britain
by Amazon.co.uk, Ltd.,
Marston Gate.